The Affordable Funeral

Going in Style, <u>Not</u> in Debt

A Consumer's Guide to Funeral Arrangements by someone outside the Funeral Industry

by

R. E. Markin, Ph.D., C.S.A.

For families everywhere, I hope this will help.

Editing assistance by Jessica Salsbury and Donald Hull

Printed in the U.S.A.

F. Hooker Press
P. O. Box 9106
Virginia Beach, VA 23450
1-757-340-7033

Fourth Edition
Thirteenth Printing 05/04

Published in Virginia Beach, Virginia by F. Hooker Press, P. O. Box 9106, Virginia Beach, VA 23450

Publisher's Cataloging-in-Publication:
(Provided by Quality Books, Inc.)

Markin, R. E.
The affordable funeral: going in style, not in debt:
A consumer's guide to funeral arrangement by someone from outside the funeral industry / by R. E. Markin –4th ed.
p.cm.
Includes bibliographical references and index
ISBN: 0-9615223-7-2 (pbk.)—ISBN: 0-9615223-9-9 (lib.)

1.Undertakers and undertaking—United States. 2. Funeral Rites and ceremonies—Economic aspects—United States. 3. Consumer education—United States. 1. Title.
HD9999 US544 2004 363.7`5`0973
QB198-1067

This edition published courtesy of a grant from the Alzheimer's Research Foundation.

Table of Contents

This book is dedicated to Alzheimer's families and caregivers everywhere. By the time Death finally arrives, you have been grieving the loss of your loved one for years. Death in a sudden flash is cruel, but death by degrees can be far worse.

Relax. It's over. You can both be at peace now.

~ Introduction ~

Hello. **You're going to die.**

That isn't an attempt to be mean or to startle you, but it's true. You ***are*** going to die, we all are. Accepting this fact and preparing for it can very much affect how those left behind will remember your departure. After our homes and our automobiles, a funeral is one of the most expensive purchases most of us will make in our lifetimes. It shouldn't be, and the very fact that you're reading these words would tend to indicate you are willing to take steps to correct this. As with anything else, it's all in ***knowing*** how.

The Death Care industry has long enjoyed relative anonymity; we know it's there, but don't talk about it much until it is absolutely necessary. Hence, most of us know little of its workings beyond what we've seen at funerals we've attended or helped arrange. The price for this ignorance can be staggering in both monetary and emotional terms and unnecessarily so.

Consider that over 2,000,000 Americans die each year and that the ***average*** funeral costs $6,000-$9,500, depending upon whose numbers you use (about $6100 per the National Funeral Directors Association [NFDA]). Now, consider the fact that the costs just quoted ***do not include*** burial plots or mausoleums, the vaults required by many cemeteries, fees for opening and closing the grave, any form of monument or headstone, nor any of several other charges that have become standard.

The total cost of a funeral with ground burial today is closer to $9,500 - $10,500, and yet most of us devote more time and care in buying a used car for Junior at half that price than to arranging a funeral. Why? We know more about used cars and there is far less emotion involved. Besides you can always change your mind about buying the car and walk off the lot, the funeral won't wait forever. You are a captive consumer, forced to do business on the funeral director's terms. Or ***are*** you?

The purpose of this work is to give you, the consumer, information you can use to make smarter decisions. It will give you a grasp of the language used and what it ***REALLY*** means, and how to go about planning a funeral without having to take out another mortgage. If you know what you're doing you can often save about half—or get twice as much for your money—and at the sums we're talking it's worth the effort.

The Structure of the Work

Since death comes at all hours and often suddenly, we will address arranging a funeral from several angles. First, we'll take the worst-case scenario wherein death has come unexpectedly. You must act quickly and make decisions that will determine not only the quality and the cost of the funeral, but also how others will perceive the family's efforts. This starts with the notification of death and covers all the basics. Subsequent sections will contain some repetition; some users will bypass early material and go directly to the section they need at the moment and I want to make sure critical areas are covered.

Next, we will look at funeral arrangement at a more leisurely pace, to examine all the options available and how to hold costs to a reasonable level, while still providing the dignity and respect we demand. This applies principally to situations in which you have advance warning of impending death and have more time to plan. The opening words of this introduction should be all the warning you need to get busy on your own arrangements.

Finally, we'll examine how one goes about planning his or her or a loved one's funeral and putting it in writing. There is a workbook you can fill-in to let survivors know what is preferred and expected. At each step we'll look at ways you can save on costs or get more for your money.

We'll also examine common ploys used to entice you to spend more than you really should and some common scams often perpetuated upon families following the loss of a loved one. Following the text there are Appendices of ***checklists*** and ***sources*** for services and information. There is also **our *Funeral Help Hotline*** phone number. Use it if you wish and we will try to help.

No one wants to dwell upon the unpleasant, but by the same token no one wants to be put in the position of having to make highly personal financial decisions in the blind. The more you know—even the more you know to ***ask*** about—the less additional stress you'll have to contend with when the time comes ... and it will come, for us all.

Our denial of that basic fact is the prime reason we tend to over-pay for funeral goods and services. We put ourselves in ***extremis*** when the time does come due to lack of preparation. Even the funeral industry admits this is a prime cause of escalating funeral costs. Let's see what denial looks like in action with a common example.

Charles is 80 years old and entered the hospital for a hip replacement. While there he contracted a serious respiratory infection and is fading fast. He, as well as his physicians and family, realizes his death is imminent. The family has been called in and Charles seizes this opportunity to try and take care of some business.

"I would like Reverend Paisley to handle my funeral service and..."

"Don't talk that way, Daddy! You're going to bounce back and be home in no time." His eldest daughter declares.

Then she launches into an upbeat monologue about what flowers are in bloom at her father's home and how nice it will be to have him back there before long. Charles listens patiently for a bit then doses off.

Charles dies the next morning and the family has lost an opportunity to ***know in detail***, from his own lips, what Charles wanted in the way of a memorial to his life. To eliminate any chance of disappointing him—or anyone else in the family—they overspend by many thousands of dollars to make sure all their bases are covered. Our culture's denial of death is demonstrated repeatedly via scenes like the above. If a loved one wants to broach the subject, do both of you an immense favor and ***listen.*** Better yet, take notes.

In the following sections you will no doubt notice some repetition and even other notes about this repetition. It is intentional. There are a few salient points I want reinforced so you'll remember.

In researching this work I contacted hundreds of funeral homes, cemeteries, monument companies, memorial societies, and crematories across the nation. Some were cooperative and free with their information and honestly want to help families at their time of need. This work is not intended to impugn the reputations of those in the industry, but rather to educate the consumer.

As with many professions that deal with people in highly emotional states, however, the funeral industry ***does*** have its share of outright scoundrels and more than a few who will charge **whatever the market will bear** for their goods and services. This is to be expected when dealing with a largely naïve consumer population. It's this naiveté I hope to eradicate, and you're a start.

Knowledge is power, read on.

I. Arranging the Unexpected Funeral

Heart attacks, strokes, auto accidents, violence, suicide, drowning; a host of forms of sudden death assails the human animal and leaves those who cared for him or her stunned. It is during this period of shock that many of the most important decisions relating to the funeral must be made by the family. The funeral director, however, deals with this sort of thing every day and has the immense psychological advantage of viewing the deceased as ***business***. For this reason, the very first rule in arranging any funeral is:

Don't go alone!

Before you approve the first item, be it releasing the body to a funeral home or identifying the remains, get someone you know and trust—and preferably someone not related-to nor otherwise emotionally involved with the deceased—and **talk**. It would help if this person has been through the process of arranging a funeral and would help even more if they've been through it ***recently***. If you're using this book in such a situation, take a moment right now to decide who this person will be, find the phone number, and **call**. If you'd like professional consumers' consultant, call (877) 427-0220 and we'll give you the number of one who can handle your area, but at the very least **have a friend by your side**.

Things will happen quickly over the first few hours, particularly if you let them. And odds are you WILL be encouraged to make decisions quickly … DON'T! While you're waiting for your friend to join you, consider this: the deceased will be no deader if you take a few minutes to make some phone calls or to confer with your friend. If you make a snap decision

("Will it be burial or cremation?") buy into a Standard Package *("I know you'd want only the VERY BEST for your loved one.")* or relinquish your decision-making power to the funeral director *("Just leave everything to us.")* however, YOU can live to regret it for years. You can 'buy' time in most cases and should do just that.

Decision #1: The Body

The first thing asked after notification of death will likely be ***"What shall we do with the body?"*** Depending on the time of day and other factors the best answer will most likely be ***"Please keep (him, her) until I can firm-up arrangements."*** This is expected from the more knowledgeable arrangers and rarely causes conflicts. Remember that **death may come suddenly, but the arrangements should follow in an orderly progression**. Haste definitely means waste in financial terms and allowing yourself to be rushed will add even more stress to an already stressful situation.

If the death occurred in a nursing home, retaining the body may not be an option since most nursing homes do not have facilities for storing bodies indefinitely and they likely have someone waiting for the bed. Most nursing homes require the family to state (via form) plans and preferences for disposition should the patient expire while in their care. This is not to say they can't hold the body for a few hours while you make arrangements, so **don't be pressured into an immediate decision**.

If pressed, simply say you need to see if the deceased has a burial plan with a funeral home and will need to verify this before authorizing the transfer. Most likely the deceased's bed is paid for through the end of the month, so don't feel bad about making them wait a few hours to fill it. In many cases, **this is where the**

greed begins. It is not without precedent for someone on the nursing home staff to have an agreement with a particular funeral home wherein they receive a monetary reward (or a nice large-screen TV for their break room, etc) for referring families of deceased residents. IF they say, "We've already made the call", you will want to speak with a higher-up and have them 'turn it off' until authorized by the family personally.

Most hospitals have refrigerated storage in the pathology unit and can retain the deceased for several days if need be, and at reasonable rates if not free of charge. This shouldn't be required but contrasted with the inflated storage charges at many funeral homes, often referred to as **Shelter of Remains** and costing hundreds of dollars, this can be a viable option. **Ask**.

Even if the death occurred at home, there is a strong likelihood the body will be transported to the local hospital or city morgue/medical examiner's office as a matter of custom or law. Unless the death was accidental, homicide, or suicide, an autopsy will not generally be performed. (Note: Some states and municipalities will require a post mortem for any death not attended by a physician.) In any event, unless you have detailed prior plans for the funeral, do not be in a hurry to move the body. You'll learn why shortly.

This time can be valuable since it delays the decision on which funeral home (if any) will receive the deceased. This can mean a difference of $1,000 or more in funeral expenses due to the ability to **shop** the various homes and avoid unnecessary or duplicate fees.

Which brings us to **Rule #2** (#1 was ***Don't Go Alone***, remember?):

Deal with ONLY ONE funeral home.

This rule is paramount. Say, for instance, the death occurred in another city or state. This is not uncommon given the medical community's propensity for transferring serious cases to the most advanced facility in the region. The hospital, coroner's office, police department, or even a minister (whoever informs you of the death) may recommend or suggest a funeral home in the city where death occurred to handle the transfer. In one way or another, this individual may be 'on the take' from the recommended funeral home. This brings us to **Rule #3**:

Do NOT agree to have the body transported to a funeral home unless that is where the funeral and burial services will take place.

Why not? You might well ask.

In each funeral arrangement there are such things as Receiving Fees, Preparation Fees, Transfer fees, Transportation Charges, and the dreaded **Non-Declinable Fees.** The non-declinable charges, also known as 'Fee For Professional Services' are fixed rates you must pay, though you get absolutely ***nothing*** in return.

By Federal Law (the Funeral Rule legislation of 1984 as amended in 1994), funeral homes are allowed to charge a fee (the Basic Fee For Professional Services) which ***includes ALL overhead and a 'reasonable' PROFIT***, and you are asked to pay this just for them being in business. All true services, such as transporting the body to the funeral home, embalming, sanitary preparations, encasing in either a shipping tray or a combination tray, and delivery to the airport for shipment, are extra. Actual fares for transportation are additional and laws require the body must be embalmed only if traveling by a **common carrier** (any transport that will also be carrying paying passengers) such as an airline. Bear in mind that hearses are **NOT** considered common carriers even if they must cross state lines and that with a few exceptions embalming is ***optional***.

It is not uncommon for non-declinable fees to run $2500 or more and here's the really tough part—there's a possibility you'll **pay this same charge again** once the body is received at the funeral home that will handle the actual funeral and burial. It's all proper and legal, just not fair. It is particularly unfair since often the funeral home will use NMS or Inman Nationwide Shipping to affect the actual services rendered, pay them their going fee of $650 or so, and pocket the rest … without ever even seeing the body!

> **An Example**: *A funeral home in a New England state received a body, embalmed it, and then transported it to the funeral home in a neighboring state that would be handling the actual services and providing the casket. The trip was less than 90 minutes by hearse.* ***The FEE was $6300.00!***

> **Another Example:** *Spring of 2002 a family in Florida called stating a great-aunt had died there and wished to be buried with her late husband in Arlington National Cemetery in Washington, DC. They'd inquired of several funeral homes locally*

> *and the best offer they had was* **$4200** *for collecting the remains, embalming, filing the necessary paperwork and transporting to the airport for transfer ... no casket, no air fare and nothing in the way of services waiting at the other end.*
>
> *We called in one of our sources in D.C. and they made one phone call. The body was embalmed, all paperwork filed, a nice casket provided, air transport provided, a hearse met the aircraft and took the body to Arlington National Cemetery where it was buried with full honors ... at a* **total cost of $2100!**

Since 1984 when Congress enacted the Funeral Rule legislation (amended in 1994)—which mandated that a casket is NOT REQUIRED for cremation, that all customers are to be given a detailed price list for services (even over the phone) and shown a price list of caskets—all sorts of things have been included under this non-declinable heading. In fact, these fees jumped nearly 30% in 1994 alone. You'll hear such things as the fee covers building overhead, rolling stock, OSHA and EPA compliance, etc. In truth the law allows the funeral home to include ALL overhead, including salaries, utilities, AND a 'reasonable' profit in their 'Basic Fee for Professional Services.

In other words, the funeral home is in the black before they provide the first funeral goods or service! To avoid duplication of charges, work with just one funeral home, the one that will ultimately handle the services, regardless of where it is in relation to the place of death. The savings can easily amount to $1000 or more.

Decision #2: Selecting the Funeral Home & Casket

Okay, the hospital called (you have your friend along side) and you've told them to hold the body until arrangements are made. Now, how do you go about this?

First, you decide what services you will need. To determine this, you must think past the funeral to the '***final disposition of remains***', which is to say, where will the body come to rest? ***Cremation? Burial? Donation? Mausoleum?*** Let's consider each since the ultimate end will dictate much in the way of what you'll need from a funeral home, if indeed you need a funeral home at all.

If you decide on **direct cremation,** which means the body is taken from the place of death directly to the crematory, call the nearest crematory or several if available. Inquire about prices and services. It is not uncommon for costs to vary widely within a given area.

A good case in point is a city I researched which had but one crematory and three funeral homes. The funeral home prices ranged from a low of $1470 to a high of $3200 for a direct cremation. The crematory stated they would perform the **same service for $600 and provide a chapel for a memorial service for free!** This could mean **a savings of $2600, just by making four calls** and is representative of prices across the nation.

As an aside, I found a charge on the funeral homes' General Price Lists (GPLs) entitled ***Cremation Charge*** (in addition to the ***Cremation Fee***) that was, probably not coincidentally, $600. They were in effect double billing and then some since the cremation cost to the funeral home was only $150!

If you decide on **direct burial** or cremation (the remains taken directly from place of death or morgue to crematory/cemetery), embalming is optional providing no common carrier transport is involved. There are only a handful of states that actually **require** embalming (and some only in cases of death from a communicable disease), so don't be bullied into this.

In fact, legislation plainly states that funeral homes are not to misrepresent state laws on embalming, but it may be up to you to stress this when the funeral home representative gets out his calculator and charge sheet. Enforcement of these laws is slack at best and I was told repeatedly that '***The State requires*** . . .' one thing or another, many of which were outright falsehoods.

Another consideration on embalming comes to us via law enforcement agencies. In the event of death by homicide, suicide or any suspicious circumstance one might want to have the body embalmed. Recent cases of decades-old homicides being solved via exhumation and DNA evidence point up an advantage of embalming (and indeed ground burial) that was not as evident in times past. Many funeral homes now take DNA samples as a matter of course during the embalming so if this is a consideration do ask.

Ground Burial

If you decide on a viewing with a delayed burial (or cremation), phone several funeral homes and ask them to have a copy of their ***General Price List, Casket Price List***, and their ***Payment Options*** waiting at their business offices for you. You might get them to give you prices over the phone, but without actually reading the fine print on services provided you'll have no idea what you are really buying at these prices. If time is of the essence, they can also fax them to you. Federal law now requires funeral home to provide these lists to anyone requesting them, but ***not*** to furnish you with a copy of the casket prices that you can keep.

Know in advance that they would rather have a ***Grief Counselor*** go over the prices with you ***to help explain your options***. These are some of the slickest salesmen around and, despite all that sympathy and understanding, they know their paycheck depends upon them *helping* ***you*** make ***their*** *right* choices.

Know also that these *professionals* typically have less formal training than a used car salesman and no licensure requirements in most states. They know only what the funeral director, or whoever trained them, has told them and that is generally limited to sales. Even licensed funeral directors who work for someone else look to commissions on 'up selling' for half or more of their paychecks.

If you go to collect the lists in person, dress casually; what you will pay is often determined by what the funeral home sales staff THINKS you can afford. This opinion is based upon your clothes, automobile, jewelry, etc. Expect to hear the names of several of your relatives if you've dealt with the home before. In particular expect to hear about the relative with the most upscale funeral. They were likely going over your family file shortly before you arrived. **Careful what financial information you divulge.**

> **An EXAMPLE**: *A lady whose husband had just died arrived at a funeral home bearing all her husband's papers related to his death, including*

a life insurance policy with a benefit of $12,000. Once finished with the 'Grief Counselor', she walked away with a $12,000.00 funeral service!
Taken from an actual letter from the widow involved.

While at the funeral home, ask to see their casket display room and catalogs/sales brochures of caskets. DON'T fall for the ***'These are the models we stock'*** or ***'Anything else will be special order and may take a while to get here.'*** dodges! Most funeral homes only stock a few models due to space considerations, but there are hundreds of models available. And even if you do select one from the floor models, odds are the actual casket will be delivered from a regional warehouse . . . the same as any 'special order' you might select which are generally available within a few hours anywhere in the country.

Jot down makes and model numbers that appeal to you (or take the sales literature on each), along with price, preferred colors and linings. Pay special attention to **gauge** numbers (often listed as 18# or 20#) in the case of steel caskets, or **weight** in the case of bronze/copper (e.g. 34 oz., etc.). You can 'shop' these around by phone later and **save yourself about 50%!**

DO NOT BUY, NOR AGREE TO BUY, A CASKET AT THIS TIME!

Not until you've read what comes **NEXT!**

COMMON PLOYS:

'Hey Diddle-Diddle, Choose what's in the Middle!'

This is the most common sales ploy, and is played at even the best-respected community funeral homes. I know, as part of my research I interviewed for sales positions with funeral homes and cemetery associations, underwent their sales training, and spoke at length with many current and ex-sales personnel. The ploy is based upon the sound marketing principal that **no one wants to seem cheap** when a loved-one is involved. It also proves that people **cannot buy what they can't see! This same technique is used when peddling 'packages' of goods and services.**

What they do is show you the top of the line first (a mahogany or bronze model, depending on how you are dressed and the model car you drive up in) which is many thousands of dollars. Next, they'll show you their 'Economy Line', that is to say a less-attractive model in steel or ash that is still quite expensive. Finally, they'll show you the model they want you to buy, say, a 16-gauge stainless steel model or a medium oak. It will be a few hundred dollars more than the ***cheap*** model, but thousands less than the top of the line. The thing you need to remember is; **all three** models they will show you are more than you need to spend.

Not only that, but the average mark-up over their cost is likely 400-700%, with mark-ups of 1400% not uncommon. There are several hundred models of perfectly lovely caskets readily available in the $700-$1400 range. Go in there with a dollar figure in mind and demand you be shown models in that range along with the color/lining options available for each.

> EXAMPLE: *An example of this sales technique I saw repeatedly was a flip chart that listed the various casket materials and the advantages of each. Fancy mahogany and bronze were at the top, copper and oak in the middle, and steel and poplar at the bottom of each page. The actual 'bottom' (or low-cost end) of the market, soft*

woods and cloth-covered pressed-board, were not even listed. Picking the 'middle range' here (Copper or Oak) would likely cost 2-4 times what a median steel casket would, and offer little in the way of additional benefits.

PLOY TWO: The Ugly Duckling

If they ***do*** have lower-priced models (most do), don't be surprised if they are in the basement, out in a dark hallway, or displayed in unflattering color combinations. Just be aware that they are available from the warehouse in the colors/linings you want, and demand to see catalogs and options.

PLOY THREE: Of *Pitch* and *Pennies*

"We don't have anything in that range in a PROTECTIVE casket."

The idea of a ***seal*** to keep out dirt, water, roots, worms, etc. can be appealing, but isn't realistic. Batesville Casket Company, the largest in the world, periodically sends out letters to funeral directors urging them to NOT make claims of 'protective qualities' for their products. As stated in the Batesville notices, the rubber gasket is not continuous (if it was, there would be difficulty opening/closing the lid for viewing) and does NOT provide protection against biological intrusion or the elements. It is also illegal for such claims of protection to be made per Federal law.

Think about it, did the ancient Egyptians depend upon airtight seals to preserve their dead? No. In fact, a seal can be detrimental to the remains in that it can promote the growth of anaerobic bacteria in the body cavity, which produce the gases that bloat the remains to the point some literally explode. This is why mausoleums require any seal on a casket be broken or removed prior to putting the remains in its crypt. This seal is pure salesmanship and an industry staple; why else would people pay extra for something that sounds good, to the uneducated, but is in fact bad? Because the funeral director pays about $12 for the rubber gasket (seal), then charges as much as $1,000 for it, that's why.

Rule #4:

A seal is important to transmissions and canned goods, but *NOT* to corpses.

Okay, you've visited and collected your lists. Take the price lists to a neutral site (your home phone will likely be ringing constantly) along with your friend. Study these price sheets and **read the fine print**. Learn what's available in terms of services and what each will cost.

There will likely be a range of ***packages*** offered with names like ***Dignity Packages*** or the ***Diplomat Package.*** This is the same ploy as banks using words like Fidelity and Trust in their names; they IMPLY something noble, upscale and trustworthy. Study these packages closely since there will likely be things included you don't want/need and others not listed that you will want/need. Pricing the services individually, ***a la carte*** if you will, then making your own offer may work much better in terms of both satisfaction and cost.

Be aware of ancillary charges such as the use of the parking lot (could be an extra $100 or more per day). Or the use of a chapel for viewing periods (which may be three- or four-hour segments amounting to several periods per day and charged by the period, often

$250.00 or more per session and up) and the use of ***common areas***, which includes lounges, the kitchen, and restrooms.

Beware of packages that are based on the number of' *Funerary* or *Memorial* Events. A viewing period, memorial service, funeral service, transfers to church or gravesite and who knows what else can constitute an ***event.*** This can be a way of generating additional charges. Should you have an extra event, say three viewing periods plus a memorial service when the package only covers ***three*** memorial events, you will be billed for the extra event. Extra events are expensive, so price them apart from the package.

You should know that what you ***call*** the service will sometimes determine the price. Use of the funeral home chapel for a ***memorial*** **service** may well go for $350, while its use for a ***funeral*** **service** is $475 though there is no set definition of either. Typically, if the body is present it's called a funeral, if absent or in the form of cremains it's a memorial service. **If any service's price is not specified, ask and get it in writing.**

Pay particular attention to any packages that suggest the prices are only valid if you purchase a casket from the funeral home. This is ILLEGAL! So is charging a ***Casket Handling Fee*** if you should buy your casket elsewhere and have it delivered to the funeral home. You can generally buy the casket and burial vault from another source at a better price, as we'll learn a bit later.

A common ploy used when the casket is purchased elsewhere, and one that was recommended in a national funeral industry magazine a few years ago, is to ***request*** that a family member be present to ***inspect*** the casket when it is delivered. They cannot require you to be present and shouldn't ask. **It is unprofessional.** Unfortunately it is also commonplace.

You may also hear veiled warnings such as "If the handles come off that 'cut-rate' casket, we can't be held responsible." The only casket I've heard of having a structural failure the past 10 years was not from an independent seller, but from a funeral home. And, it was an upscale Batesville oak model at that. To be honest with Batesville, the casket in question was a *standard* size (rather than over sized) unit into which a funeral home had stuffed a 400+ pound man. To make matters worse, the staff was trying to lift the casket manually from both ends and the strain was too much. A handle did, in fact, break loose. Caskets are fairly standardized in terms of construction, due to the simple fact most of them come from a handful of pressing plants in North America.

Many funeral homes are family-owned and are therefore more flexible in their terms. They would likely forego an extra $500-1000 in additional profit on a casket rather than lose $4500 worth of services, so do mention if you think the casket or burial vault is priced too high. As often as not, when a family calls us for a price comparison, the funeral home just gives the family the unit at the lower price rather than risk losing the family's trust and future business.

Also, be aware that big corporations like SCI (Service Corporation International), Stewarts, and Carriage Services own about a quarter of all the funeral homes in the United States, and their prices and policies are pretty much dictated by corporate headquarters. This means far less flexibility in pricing. Ask during your initial phone call if the home is owned by one of the large corporate 'consolidators' and factor this into your decision when selecting.

This decision could save you 25-40% since some of these corporate giants report profits per funeral several times higher than the independently owned homes. Per Father Henry Wasielewski, a Catholic priest who has dedicated much of the past four decades to revealing the excesses of the funeral industry, SCI's prices average about 35% more than other funeral homes in market surveys across the nation. The other corporation-owned homes are similar.

A few more words about caskets

Of the total funeral cost, nearly HALF is spent on the casket. This figure is hotly disputed in an industry that is quick to show you a little pie chart from a study that shows the casket accounts for only 14%. Of course that pie chart is from the front page of a newspaper back in **1972**! From what I've seen and heard, the casket is indeed the major single expense. It needn't be.

More than any other facet of the funeral business, the casket is routinely subject to outrageous price inflation on behalf of the funeral homes. By ***outrageous*** mark-ups I mean 300%, 500%, perhaps even 1500% for some items, with the national average falling somewhere around 400%.

Caskets and vaults are actually quite reasonable from the manufacturers. And, there are funeral homes and 'casket stores' out there that can provide what you want at a reasonable price. You just cannot count on ***your*** funeral home being one of them.

> EXAMPLE: *For a particularly-upscale casket I priced along the East Coast, prices ranged from a low of $12,800 (in Southeastern Virginia) to a*

> *high of nearly $70,000 (in Washington, D.C., 150 miles away). The mean price for this casket was $25,000, and each funeral home paid exactly the same wholesale price ($11,800) for it. The range of lower- and mid-range casket prices runs this way, too, with mark-ups from the sublime (rarely) to the ridiculous (routinely).*
>
> ANOTHER EXAMPLE: *The 'alternative container' used in cremation amounts to a glorified cardboard box. At funeral homes I saw these routinely priced at $65-$110, though some went as high as $465 (on the West Coast). After a little research I learned that this $465 is what a bundle of 50 of the same boxes cost retail. Is that a coincidence? The same container is available from some state cremation societies for under $20! Do the math and you'll find markups of 650% to 4650%*

You may also hear them use the term ***disposal of the remains*** of your loved-one, as in, "*This wood composite box would be adequate for the disposal of the remains, but we can't guarantee anything about it.*" anytime you mention selecting a more reasonably priced casket. Okay, burial, cremation, donation, whatever, actually ***is*** the disposal of the remains. Anything short of mummification or taxidermy is. They know, and you should know too, that ***disposal*** sounds far more heartless than ***disposition*** ... **don't get taken to the cleaners over semantics**. Word games are big in their marketing scheme.

The Materials & Terminology

Steel caskets are listed by **gauge**, which is to say the thickness of the steel used with the lower the gauge the thicker the steel. ***Gauge*** is the number of sheets required to make a stack one-inch thick. As an example shotguns are stated by the thickness of their barrels such as 12-gauge, 20-gauge, etc. You'll see 16-Gauge, 18-Gauge, 20-Gauge and 22-Gauge steel caskets commonly listed. The difference between the top-of-the-line and average is the difference between the thickness of a car bumper and the thickness of a STOP sign. **You will be encouraged to go for the lower gauge for its increased *security*.** This is impractical or misleading for two reasons.

First, consider that the casket itself will likely be enclosed in a vault of concrete or metal, so there is no load-bearing requirement. Second, realize that since our population is increasing at an alarming rate. There is a very real likelihood that in less than 100 years most cemeteries will have been confiscated for development or crops, just as they have been in the Far East and Europe. When this happens the bodies are dug up and cremated, so there's little advantage to a thicker gauge casket, except in profits or commission to whoever is selling it.

In the course of our study one of the most common remarks from family members was that they wished they'd spent MORE on the monument and less on the casket. Since the monument is all that remains visible following the service this is probably good advice.

Steel caskets start around $600.00, for a 20-gauge model with crepe lining. The national average price (per my data) is closer to $2200.00 for 20-gauge and $3100.00 for 16-gauge, with Stainless steel models going for $3,000.00 or more. Steel models are the most-popular of all caskets and, as such, often have a hefty mark-up that puts them at the *'... for a few dollars more you can have copper or mahogany.'* level. **Bait-and-Switch is a popular ploy** throughout the industry, so watch for it.

Copper and bronze are the casket elite, starting at about $3500 and progressing rapidly to $10,000 and more. Much, MUCH MORE! The absolute top of the line can run you $30,000.00 or more, depending on what part of the country you live in and how gullible you are. Copper and Bronze caskets are listed in weight categories, such as 32-ounce and 48-ounce, representing the weight per square foot of material. The key selling points to these caskets are that they don't rust and they're the top-of-the-line, in other words, **snob appeal**.

You may also be told they offer superior protection, better seals, and other things. They don't. Nature will, in the end, have its way.

Wooden caskets are made of mahogany, walnut, cherry, oak, maple, or poplar. There are also some nice models made of pine and ash, but you're not likely to see them or to know of their existence at all unless you specifically ask. Pine, by the way, is ***not*** a bottom-of-the-line option; pine caskets can cost thousands.

Wooden caskets are beautiful works of art, but offer nothing in the way of ***protection*** from moisture, unless you're also willing to spring an extra $1,750 or more for the optional copper or glass liner.

Since wood is porous, the much-vaunted 'seal' is not even used. If you opt for a lower-end wooden casket, expect a strong sales pitch for a more expensive burial vault. These, too, are subject to horrendous mark-ups and, despite all the claims of protection;

many models have holes in the bottom to keep them from floating!

Wood models run from about $2,000 for poplar to $10,000 and up for mahogany. Composite board can start around $400 and even the least expensive model can be draped with a flag or augmented with floral arrangements to good advantage.

You should know that the more expensive woods are available in both veneer and 'planked' or solid. Veneer mahogany, for instance, is a thin sheet of mahogany (1/28th of an inch thick) glued to plywood. Veneer caskets **should** cost less than solid or 'planked', but unless you know to ask you may pay full price.

For arrangement budget purposes, figure about $900-$1600 for a nice wooden or steel casket and let the funeral director find you the options in this range. If he can't, call us. We know of some nice wooden caskets that are quite reasonable and readily available, starting at under $1,000 delivered.

I mentioned earlier that you should take down model, color, lining, hardware options, etc ... in order to 'shop' the cost of the casket. Each casket company makes a version of the most popular models. Probably a dozen models account for 90% of all burials, so you don't have to worry about availability, even from a casket store.

We have a list of reasonable casket providers who stock most brands and can deliver virtually any of them within hours to the funeral home of your choice. Find the model and color you like, check the prices available locally, then call the **Funeral Help Program Hotline at 877-427-0220** to get a national cost comparison and/or alternate sources for the same product.

Just state the make, model, and color desired (along with interior options if available), the funeral home price, your phone number and the city where the burial is to take place. If we have another source that can significantly beat this price, you'll be called by the supplier to arrange payment and have it delivered. It won't be wholesale, but the mark-up will be more like 40% than 400% (in many cases, \$50- \$200 above cost) and that alone could cut the cost of the funeral by thousands while still providing everything you want.

Decision Time: Your Options

Cremation

In some areas of the United States, cremation has overtaken burial as the most common disposition of the remains. This is particularly true in the case of up-scale neighborhoods. In ritzy Marin County, California, for instance, about 70% of all families choose cremation. In the Pacific Northwest, where the land is too beautiful to squander on sterile fields of stone, about half of all families elect cremation. On a national average, somewhere between twenty and thirty percent of all families elect cremation and there's several good reasons why.

We are a more mobile society these days, more prone to pack up our belongings and move to a more pleasant climate, a better job, etc. This makes visitation more challenging and expensive. With *cremains*, as the ashes of the deceased are known, you can pack up your ancestors, too. From a purely economic standpoint, cremation will cost 50% to 80% less than burial.

Aesthetically, the ashes can be scattered in a favorite place or at-sea, from an aircraft or boat, or retained in an urn. There's even one outfit that advertises they can shoot cremains out into space, for a hefty fee! Others will convert your loved one’s cremains into a touchstone, paperweight, coral reef or even a diamond. Perhaps every bit as important as what you get with cremation is what you can do without.

Things you WON'T need if you elect cremation are:

*A casket (if you desire a viewing, most funeral homes have rental caskets with changeable liners available) ($150-UP, a savings of $600-$10,000)
*A burial plot or mausoleum ($500-$5,000+) unless you elect to have the ashes buried in a cemetery or placed in a niche.
*A vault/grave liner for the grave ($500-$2500 and WAY UP) Some cemeteries require 'cremains vaults', which is a pure price gouge since there's no real concern with the urn collapsing.
*A headstone ($650-Up) Granted, for niches some form of plaque will be required, but it is generally less than a grave marker.
*The cost of opening and closing a grave ($300-$1500+)
*Pallbearers
*A Hearse ($100-$500) and/or Limousines from chapel to graveside

For dispersal at-sea, from an aircraft, or on foreign soil, see Appendix A for sources that perform these services as well as U. S. Navy and Coast Guard contacts. The **Neptune Society**, which has chapters in several large cities and advocates cremation and scattering at-sea, **is a *for-profit organization* and is affiliated with one of the large corporations.** For a cost-effective cremation option in your area, phone **1-800-CREMATE.**

Donation

Another option is **donation** of the remains to medical science. Funeral directors detest this option, by the way, and some are not above telling falsehoods about it. Several have told the families of prospective donors that the medical schools are refusing bodies just now, due to a glut. Or they'll say that "Since your loved one was ... [at an advanced age, a victim of cancer, a rather mundane heart failure, male or female, over-weight, *pick an excuse*!] medical schools and teaching hospitals aren't interested and won't take them." This is not without an element of truth.

I have yet to speak with a medical school or teaching hospital that had more cadavers than it needed. In fact, just the opposite is generally true. They are actively seeking donations, and are even dealing with ***Cadaver Brokers*** to get them. There are things that will render a body less useful to science, however. Paramount among these is organ donation, morbid obesity and autopsy (which can inhibit the embalming process), but generally these institutions welcome any help along these lines that is offered.

You should check with the receiving institution early because some will require the FAMILY to pay for embalming and transportation. Embalming for **preservation** is different from the standard embalming for **presentation** and can cost more. You may also find yourself paying the funeral home's Fee For Professional Services, an extra Transportation Fee, and who knows what else! You can consult with other institutions and find one that is more consumer-friendly.

Another nice thing about this option is that, generally after one year, **the cremated remains are returned to the family ... free**. As an option that offers the opportunity to help humanity and to minimize funeral expenses, donation to medical science is the ultimate.

There are companies out there that will actually PAY for bodies. The legal and moral aspects of this are constantly debated, but a recent case indicates there is a market for human remains. Typically the body is parceled out with organs going to several entities, limbs and extremities elsewhere, bones and ligaments to yet others. Since it is illegal to sell body parts for transplantation, the body still goes primarily to research. As with donation to an institution, the cremated remains are typically returned to the family within a year or two and these companies usually pay for embalming, transport, etc.

Ground Burial/Mausoleum

For burial you will need all the things mentioned above that are exclusions for cremation, starting with a burial plot. The final question I asked of each funeral home I contacted was, ***'What one thing would you warn your patrons about that could save them money on funeral expenses?'*** The most common two answers were, "***Don't let emotions over-run common sense when buying funeral goods and services***." and, a close second, "***Beware of cemetery salesmen, they generally work on a commission-only basis and consider it a personal failure if they let you out of their office without signing something***."

It goes without saying that funeral homes that own, or are directly affiliated with and participate in the profits of, a cemetery should be approached with due care (see notes on corporate entities who own hundreds of cemeteries as well as funeral homes). A solid tip that can save you thousands is, check your local newspaper and those little papers filled with nothing but classified ads you'll find near the check-out lines at your supermarket. The latter of these go by names like ***The Thrifty Nickel***, ***Ad Sack***, ***Marketplace***, ***Trading Post***, etc.

You'll find crypts and burial plots listed under ***Cemetery*** or ***Burial Lots,*** either by themselves or near the ***Real Estate*** listings. While the cost of these second-hand plots is usually very reasonable, some precautions are in order. Be certain you check for outstanding balances at the cemetery concerned and that there isn't an exclusive clause stating ownership is not transferable without the cemetery's approval. Church and religious-affiliated cemeteries often require their council or board (or ***Chevra Ka"disha***, in the case of

Jewish cemeteries) approve any sales or transfers, even among family members. You'll also want to make sure a 'marker permit' is included if you wish to purchase a monument.

Read the deed, bill of sale or title. Plots are often sold ***subject to current conditions and policies***, not necessarily what is stated on the bill of sale. For instance, say you want to buy a plot that was last sold in 1968. At the time, each unit was sold with the condition that for each burial the grave would be opened and closed for a sum of $50. The current price for this service is $500. You will likely pay the $500, not what is stated on the 1968 document. Before purchasing, check with the cemetery for current policies, prices and conditions to know what you are actually getting.

Your funeral director likely keeps the phone numbers and basic price information about all the cemeteries in the area and can provide you with guidance in this direction. This list can serve as a good starting point for comparing prices. I found it much easier to get reliable information over the phone than in person, not to mention the fact that, as salesmen go, these cemetery guys are persuasive! If you show up in person you will receive the full sales treatment before you can leave.

As a rule, the funeral director does NOT receive a commission for any sales he steers to the cemetery, but this may not be the case when the funeral home and cemetery are under the same proprietor or are corporate-owned. Likewise, you may find that members of the clergy are given finder's fees for steering people to funeral establishments. Also, be wary of any information you might see in the waiting room at a hospice, since funeral directors and cemetery owners sit on the Board of Directors of many hospice programs across the nation.

MEMORIAL SOCIETIES

For information on holding funeral costs down, you can consult your local Memorial Society or chapter of The Funeral Consumers Alliance. These are membership organizations that monitor funeral prices in their area and sometimes negotiate with funeral businesses for price breaks for their members. If their information is kept current they can be great sources. Check on the Internet for a chapter nearby; ***www.funerals.org***

VETERANS

Some veterans and their immediate families can be buried in national cemeteries, including the main one in Arlington, Virginia. These burial plots are free, but transportation of the remains is left to the family unless the deceased died on active duty. In **Appendix A** you will find the numbers to call and the documentation required to qualify for of this entitlement. Most national cemeteries also have columbaria or niches for cremains, should cremation be elected. You should also know that many states have veterans' cemeteries also.

Having served with both the U.S. Army and the Navy, I have attended numerous ceremonies at national and state cemeteries over the years and found them to be among the most reverential and memorable of all. The service men and women attending these ceremonies are professional in their treatment of 'one of their own', providing an overall aura of abiding respect. There is even the option of an aircraft fly-by with the 'Missing

Man' formation, if an air facility is nearby and the training schedule permits. It never hurts to ask.

BOTH Cremation AND Burial

There's no rule that says you can't have both burial and cremation. Many people elect cremation and have their ashes (or at least some of them) interred in the cemetery with their family. There's a complete line of products for this and, as mentioned earlier, some cemeteries have anticipated this by requiring the use of a ***cremains vault***! These little hutches cost only a fraction of what the full-sized units run, but can still be a considerable expense if you get carried away. Bear in mind that all you're ***containing*** is a few pounds of ground bone. Most any container will serve this function. A nice vase, ginger jar or cigar humidor works well and can cost a fraction of what these 'made for the purpose' urns and vaults will run.

Just as an example of the options cremation allows, I know of one individual who has stipulated in his plans that a 'pinch' of his ashes be sprinkled at a national cemetery and another pinch be buried alongside his family' graves in a community cemetery (with a full-sized monument). The bulk of his ashes are to be scattered at-sea.

This person is myself. Having lived in numerous states and countries, as well as spending many years at-sea, it seems the best overall option. Besides, there's something romantic about returning to the sea, there to become a part of every wave that breaks on every shore, and every drop of rain that falls. It appeals to me far more than eternity in a box, but to each his or her own.

Funeral Brokers & Consultants

A relatively new phenomenon that has grown out of the catering and florist industries starting on the West Coast is the Funeral Services Broker or Consultant. This started with florists deciding that, since they were taking orders for floral acknowledgments anyway, they could simultaneously print addressed Thank You cards at a nominal fee and relieves the family of the bother. The more knowledgeable of these began offering advice and the consulting business was born. Now true professionals are in this field.

Funeral consultants may offer cost comparisons on local funeral homes and cemeteries, offer to negotiate on your behalf for a burial plot or crypt, or even handle the arrangement visit in your stead. Be sure to ask if they have any affiliation with the cemeteries involved. Their data may be tainted if they receive a commission on sales they generate and you need to know this up-front.

As of this writing not many of the funeral directors I spoke with care to work with funeral brokers. They see them as a threat to profits or an unnecessary layer of bureaucracy that can add tension to the proceedings by coming between them and the family. This is true of consultants who take too active a part in the actual conduct of the ceremonies.

Where consultants do serve a beneficial purpose is in offering cost comparisons and steering the family away from redundant charges. They can interpret each step of the arrangement process into plain language and explain your options at each step.

Having someone on your side that deals with this daily will be worth more than the consultant's compensation as a rule. Our trained consultants (Affordable Funeral Consultants) are mostly retired elder law attorneys, hospice workers, nurses and ministers. Many do consulting as an adjunct to their profession and others do consulting as their main job. Some may even offer their services for free. They offer a simple guarantee, ***"We'll save you at least triple our fee, or our services are FREE."***

Opening and Closing the Grave

This is one service it pays to know a bit about. Charges vary across the nation. In fact, some grave openings/closings are included in the price of the plot, though some maintain this service only accrues to the original purchaser. An interesting fact emerged from my research; ***fees can vary widely according to the day of the week or even the time of day the opening or closing is performed.***

An example is a cemetery that charges a flat $550 to open and close (dig a hole, fill it in) a grave during the week. That figure assumes opening/closing the grave during ***normal weekday work hours.*** Therein lies the rub! Normal work hours at this cemetery are from 9 a.m. to 3 p.m. Monday through Thursday. Outside these narrow hours charges are as follows:

- M-Th prior to 9 a.m. or after 3 p.m.--- $ 750
- Friday -- 995
- Saturday before 1 p.m. ----------------- 1495
- After 1 p.m. on Saturday, anytime Sunday or on any religious, state or National holiday ------------------------- 1995

Knowing this price structure in advance could save $1000 or more. Since cemeteries do NOT fall under the Funeral Rule Legislation, they are not required to furnish a price list nor even a detailed bill. The only way to know fees for certain is to ask. Sometimes it will pay to compare charges for opening/closing the grave between the cemetery association and the funeral home, if both offer this service.

In rural areas you might be ahead of the game just phoning a backhoe service and getting a quote since they often do the actual digging regardless of who receives the payment. You should also be aware that some of the larger burial vault companies, such as Wilbert, ‘set’ their vaults into the grave for free. More than a few have also been charged for this by the cemetery or funeral home.

The Case for Mausoleums

While we're here, let's consider mausoleums. We've all seen them in old movies and perhaps at the more posh memorial parks and, likely as not, figured they were reserved for the particularly wealthy. Perhaps not, considering the total outlay of the alternative ground burial.

Mausoleums sell for around $2500 per space and up, way up. Just as was the case with cremation, the true value lies in what you can do without.

Items you won't have to pay for with a mausoleum.

*No opening/closing of the grave ($500-$2000) [although there will likely be a 'sealing', 'encrypting', or similar charge]

*No Vault/Grave Liner ($500-$2500 and UP)

*No Marker/Monument ($650-UP, and again there will be something similar, though generally much less expensive)
*No Burial Plot ($500-Up)

All things considered, mausoleums are probably a good buy. This is particularly true in the case of those (the deceased or family) who have an aversion to the thought of being buried. Mausoleums offer a permanence to rival the ground burial, without the future problems of grave collapse or roots penetrating the vault. They offer superior protection from moisture and have always been the choice of those for whom money was no object (e.g. the pyramids of Egypt, the Tomb of the Unknowns, the Taj Mahal, etc.).

Mausoleums allow visitation in all weather conditions and some offer a chapel and/or a visiting lounge. With industry giants like Gibraltar™ (now owned by SCI) leading the way with pre-sold units built as demand dictates, look for these 'condominiums of the dead' to increase in popularity, particularly since the cost of a routine ground burial is often as much as or more than a crypt.

Here is an interesting note on mausoleums. Say you were an adventurous sort who decided to sell mausoleum crypts on a 'pre-need' basis and then build the mausoleum to accommodate the number of crypts sold. Per some state laws, you wouldn't have to even ***begin*** construction on the mausoleum for up to eight years ***after*** its capacity has sold out!

Now, if this set-up strikes you as a golden opportunity to be left holding a useless piece of paper when your time comes while some shifty entrepreneur is off sunbathing in the islands, we're in agreement! Know what you're getting, go see it, and don't be overly trusting of anyone until the sucker is actually built. Until the building is above ground, future inhabitants will be stored below ground and many of the benefits will be lost.

Vaults and Grave Liners

Most cemeteries now require some form of outer container. These are metal or concrete shells into which caskets are placed in the grave. The rationale behind them depends upon which salesman you listen to. It's to keep moisture out of the casket (which is also sealed, as a rule, but could float up in the case of major ground water). Or to prevent the surface of the grave from collapsing once the casket deteriorates. Or it functions to prevent the weight of the dirt from crushing the casket (an unlikely immediate event, but a good sales ploy). What they actually provide is a level surface for ease of mowing and a solid profit center for the cemetery.

As with caskets, it is illegal to tout the protective merits of a burial vault. It is ludicrous to do so, in fact, considering many have holes in their bottoms to prevent the whole thing from floating up. They will delay the casket collapse, however, and given the weaker alloys used in caskets these days they are probably necessary.

Tree roots can penetrate at-will and, according to numerous sources within the industry, if you want a vault that is truly waterproof you'll need to spend several thousands of dollars ... perhaps as much as $10,000! Here we're talking the deluxe, seamless bronze vaults with glass lining and even these are not impervious to roots.

The thing I find interesting about vaults and grave liners is, we have our clergymen quote that old "***... ashes-to-ashes and dust-to-dust***" spiel, then go to extreme lengths and expense to keep that from happening! Nature won't allow this, of course, and given time we'll all return to our elements no matter how much we spend on vaults and the like. Be reasonable.

Here's another example of how knowing the language could save you money. Price a vault and a grave ***liner***. Both of these units accomplish, or fail to accomplish, the same things and yet the price of the vault may be several times that of the grave liner. Sales training said this was because the word ***vault*** just sounds more substantial than ***liner***. This comes under the heading 'perceived value' and in this case is erroneous. Most liners we encounter in life are made of plastic or cloth, while vaults are concrete and steel. Liners in the funeral industry are usually made of concrete and steel. Do ask for a grave liner if an outer container is required and you'll save $500 or so.

The cost to the funeral home or cemetery association runs from about $150 for a concrete liner to $500-1000 (or more) for a fancier metal variety. Retail, which is to say your cost, will run from $400 to $2000 for the low end of the spectrum and all the way up to $20,000 for the more exotic metals and fancy sealing systems.

An interesting case I encountered was a cemetery that sold a standard concrete vault for $495. At the top of their line was a seamless bronze model with a glass lining for about $15,000.00 which clients were shown first. Then the salesman would say,

"***I do happen to have three remaining 'Bronze XXX' models, which have been discontinued, and I***

can let you have one for $1495.00. They feature polymer handles, and a chemical matrix seal along the lip."

The 'Bronze XXX' model was actually a $495 concrete model ***spray-painted*** a bronze color, the 'polymer handles' were **nylon straps** embedded in the concrete, and the ***chemical matrix seal*** was a few penny's-worth of pitch dribbled along the edges of the lid! That's not much for your extra $1000 so beware.

You can compare price quotes from the cemetery association and the funeral home. There are some nice models out there for under $300; you just have to know where to look. If you are buying a burial plot, you might make a deal on a grave liner or vault being included. Never hurts to ask, right?

Monuments

You can spend as much or as little as you want on headstones, markers, etc ... The median price falls around $1,200 nationwide and it is customary to wait until things have leveled-off to a less emotional state before ordering one. This also gives the grave time to settle. Some savvy cemeteries require a specific type of stone or bronze plaque and, no surprise here, provide them at a set cost or make them a part of the burial plot sales 'package'. This is another thing to consider when selecting a burial plot, and a hurdle in getting a better price elsewhere.

I have spoken with several stone companies over the past couple of years and compared prices and purchasing trends. Some interesting points surfaced. Monuments come in three forms, the standard gray granite, colored granite and/or marble, and the bronze plaque (usually mounted to a stone base). Buyers over age 60 tend to buy traditional gray granite, while buyers in their 50s or younger opt for the colored stones. The bronze is something few elect of their own accord, but rather is often required by the cemetery association to both ease maintenance (by being able to mow over these flush-mounted plaques) and to pad their pockets.

It is important to note that, unlike all the other expenses of the funeral (which end up either below the ground, in a crypt, up in smoke, or in the undertaker's pocket), the monument is a lasting tribute for all to see. For this reason in particular, some care should be exercised in selecting a monument.

Granite is preferable to marble in most instances because marble tends to oxidize and wear-away or discolor more readily than the harder granite. Granite comes in three grades; Light (which is the least expensive but is most likely to show pollution or stains), Medium (a good grade), and Dark (the most dense and stable).

On several occasions I received quotes that were virtually identical, yet were based on the entire range of grades including something called 'Monument Grade', which is actually the minimum quality. Know which grade you're getting and take that into account when you consider price. The mere fact that you are aware there are multiple grades will make you less likely to be taken, so do ask.

Where you buy your monument in the U.S. will also play a part in its price. South of the Mason-Dixon Line, for instance, most stone is Georgia Granite. North of this fabled line the stone will likely be Barre Granite from Barre, Vermont. The difference in quality? None. The difference in price? Perhaps as much as 50% due to Vermont companies having to pay union wages and higher shipping costs. You can specify Georgia Granite when ordering and, for the same quality stone, likely save some money. Any stone with the trademark ***Rock Of Ages™*** will likely cost 25-35% more than an equivalent stone without it. It' not worth the extra expense.

Another important factor with monuments is the installation. A common complaint among stone companies is that, if ***they*** sell the monument, the cemetery association makes them dig a deep footing and pour concrete prior to setting the stone. If, on the other hand, the cemetery association sells the stone, they just dig a little hole, scatter some gravel, and drop the stone in it to settle or tilt as it will. How true this is will vary with the association and can only be determined by personal inspection.

Some monument companies place little metal tags on each stone, to identify the company. You'll find these to one side of the marker, or mounted to the base. The presence of this tag speaks a certain amount of pride on behalf of the company and makes it easier for descendants to locate the company in the future should there be a problem. I have encountered more than one monument company that has been around for over a century yet still maintains stones set by their great-grandfathers… often free of charge!

Selecting a Monument

A good way to select a stone and a company to provide it is to get out to the cemeteries and look around. Check the quality of workmanship, contrast of lettering, condition of the stone itself (pollution erosion or staining, is it level or has it sunk into the ground?) and look for those little tags identifying the company.

Once you have an idea of what you want, drive around to the various companies.

Here's a hint provided by one of the older stone companies in Virginia; ***take a real good look at the samples yard***! An average samples yard (stones in various shapes and colors often displayed on the front lawn of the stone company) contains between $25,000 and $60,000 worth of monuments. What you want to see is a lot of monuments WITHOUT NAMES AND DATES engraved upon them. Why? Because these engraved 'samples' are probably **mistakes** the company has made on actual orders! Granted, all companies make mistakes from time-to-time, but $50,000 worth staring at you at one time does not bode well.

While we're speaking of mistakes on monuments, as a rule the lighter the color of the stone the deeper it must be engraved for contrast. The deeper the engraving the more difficult and/or expensive it will be to grind off the error and re-engrave. If it's too deep, there are only two options; fill the engraving with epoxy and re-engrave it or discard the stone (sample yard) and start over.

Which option is taken is often determined by who is deemed to be at-fault for the error. If the purchaser (family member or funeral home/cemetery association) gives the stone company incorrect information, then the company is not responsible for the error and will charge extra for correcting same. If the stone company screws up the purchaser should have his choice of remedies.

Bear in mind that epoxy may discolor in a few years and ask to see a weathered example before opting for this cure. Here you can see the benefit of dealing directly with the stone company, both to avoid errors to begin with and to have a say in how they are corrected should errors occur.

Veterans are entitled to a monument or plaque from the VA, see Appendix A for the address/phone number and information you'll need to provide. These monuments are quite nice, simplistic, and of high quality. There are at least four models from which to choose, including a bronze plaque that is acceptable to virtually all cemetery associations.

Notice that part of many cemetery packages relating to perpetual care include statements to the effect that "***... monuments may need shimming every few years to account for settling. This will vary with the soil at the installation site***." If the monument is installed correctly, it won't. This is another way cemetery associations pad their incomes (Perpetual Maintenance) and why they may not use concrete footings when installing their own stones ... to insure they ***will*** tilt or settle.

Bronze Plaques

Cast bronze is sold by the square inch. A common ploy to bilk money from unsuspecting customers is to cite a reasonably low price per square inch, then charge for the area of the base stone as well. This will be covered later in depth, but for now suffice it to say you should know what you are buying before you agree to anything.

Vandalism & Monuments

It occasionally happens, some idiot with a sledge damages monuments. You may find such things covered by, of all things, your **homeowners insurance!** Ask your agent.

Monument Technology

Monument technology is advancing with the advent of lasers and computer-augmented plotters, etc. If you can conceive it, someone can make it. Monuments bearing color photos or grayscale etchings are commonplace and now there are even 'talking monuments' that allow the departed to welcome visitors. If you have something special in mind, be sure to ask. You might be pleasantly surprised at what is available.

Funeral Services

The least expensive mode of funeral today is direct cremation (or donation to science) with a memorial service at a church, meeting hall, bar or someone's home. All told, this can run as little as $750 for a nice send-off. If the deceased is a qualified veteran and you'd like the ashes dispersed at-sea, you can contact the nearest U. S. Navy Medical Center and ask to speak with Decedent Affairs, or contact the folks listed in Appendix A. There is no charge, but there is generally a wait until a ship is made available for this and you are responsible for getting the cremains to the ship. This can be done via UPS, Federal Express, Parcel Post, or any other traceable means.

If burial is preferred, a direct burial (which does not require embalming) followed by a memorial service is the next least expensive option. One should bear in mind the adage that funerals are actually for the living when considering what services and good to purchase.

It is ironic that, contrary to what one might expect, the most expensive funerals are those arranged by and for the less educated blue-collar workers, while **the more educated and affluent tend toward modest ceremonies and cremation**. The general feeling among the upper crust seems to be, “You can’t take it with you, but you can certainly leave as much of it as possible to your heirs and family.”

Conversely, many of more modest means seem to think their life insurance or death benefit should be spent on one glorious event to mark their passing. As always, it is a matter of personal preference, and the ‘spend more on the monument than the casket’ applies.

As mentioned earlier, some mausoleums have chapels. This can provide a nice place for the service that is not as weather-dependent as a standard ground burial and, since many also have niches provided for ashes within the mausoleum, serve well for pre- or post-cremation services, too. As far as the actual ceremony goes, the diversity of religious and cultural traditions forbid my going into detail on each one. Suffice it to say whatever you want, you can have. Get with your minister, priest, etc ... and decide what is required and/or desired.

Funeral Home Fees

Funeral homes break down their charges under several broad headings:

Fee For Professional Services:

This **may** include a few basic services, but is usually used to cover overhead and profit, providing NOTHING in return for your money. (Remember?) Do not, however, take this figure as the be-all end-all of your comparison when shopping for a funeral home. One local establishment (Virginia Beach) has the lowest FFPS in the area, but more than makes up for it with inflated embalming/prep and transportation costs.

Use of Facilities & Staff:

Includes use of staff and chapel for viewing, for the funeral ceremony, or for a memorial service. Also ***may*** include graveside services and tent if needed. Don't think you'll save money by having the service at a church because typically the fee for staff to transfer and attend said services is the same as the use of the funeral home chapel.

Embalming & other sanitary preparations:

This is about what it sounds like and includes cosmetics and restoration (may be an hourly charge), bathing and dressing the deceased and encasketing. Embalming is not actually ***required*** by law, in most cases, but if you intend to have a delayed burial (perhaps to give distant relatives time to travel) or a viewing you'll probably want it.

Virtually all funeral homes have both air conditioning and refrigerated storage so embalming isn't as critical as it was a few decades ago. There are two forms of embalming, for presentation and for preservation. For a viewing the more superficial 'presentation' type procedure is performed which delays natural processes (decomposition) by a week or two. Embalming for longer term 'preservation', say for medical research, involves more intense invasion of tissues with preservative fluids that may result in an unpleasant odor.

Aesthetically, the injection of reddish-hued fluid tends to give the body a more ‘pink’ and lifelike appearance. The addition of cosmetics to visible skin and the use of rose-colored lighting enhance this. Do not think you are preserving the body forever, as that simply isn’t the case. In dry, warm climates, the body may desiccate (dry out) over time as in the case of naturally occurring mummies, assuming there is air circulation. In less optimum climates the body may completely disintegrate to a skeleton over a few months or years. This is why mausoleums have the casket lid open slightly and circulates warm air through the compartments, to aid in desiccation.

As of this writing, embalming is actually required by less than ten states. Don't be snowed into buying a service package because someone says 'That includes the embalming, which is required by law.' If the body is to be shipped by common carrier it does have to be embalmed, so if the body is shipped in from out-of-state by air there's no need to do it again upon arrival. You might be amazed at the number of people who pay for embalming and a fancy oak, cherry, or mahogany casket, only to have the deceased cremated within hours ... casket included!

Several establishments told me that state law requires a burial vault. This is an outright fabrication. The cemetery association often requires them, but not by any legislation. This brings up a point you should consider; many of the ***sales personnel are often neither licensed nor formally trained; they know only what they are told by their bosses***. They are sincere in what they say and tend to quote specific figures for comparison whenever asked.

Unfortunately, on more than one occasion I found the figures being quoted were from studies published by the NFDA two or more decades ago! In the years subsequent, these figures and percentages have nearly tripled and their proportional relationships have changed radically. If there is ***any*** question, don't be shy about asking to deal with a funeral ***director*** rather than a salesman.

Transportation:

Transfer of deceased to the funeral home, to a church or to the cemetery all have set fees. You can also expect fees for use of a limousine(s), other automotive equipment (flower van, etc.) and additional mileage charges outside a fixed range. You may be charged for a 'lead car' or 'service vehicle', which is a fancy way of saying 'the car in which the funeral director and/or his staff rides'.

Receiving or Transfer Fees

If the body is coming from another funeral home and is already embalmed, the fee for receiving is a way the funeral home can charge you (or recuperate) for services rendered elsewhere. There will still be an additional fee for going to the airport and collecting the body. Receiving charges are largely greed if you paid the other funeral home to do the prep. If you did the smart thing and coordinated everything through the receiving funeral home, the receiving fee merely compensates for transfer services rendered.

There are some items the receiving home will need to attend to, of course. The receiving establishment usually performs cosmetic work, final dressing, encasketing and perhaps topical restoration, though most of this will be billed ***in addition*** to the receiving charge.

Likewise, if you do not coordinate transfer of the body through the ultimate establishment where the actual services will be rendered, you will also pay a 'Forwarding Fee' which can run from several hundred to a few thousand dollars. This is why we emphasize dealing with ***only ONE*** funeral home. You pay one fee, not two, and you actually get something for your money.

Charges for Merchandise Selected:
This includes the casket or alternative burial container, vault or liner, cremation urn, clothing and other merchandise. Except in the case of the economically challenged, families usually provide clothing for the deceased rather than buying it from the funeral home. Still, the funeral home does offer appropriate apparel, usually at a reasonable price, though one really must question the industry selling a million dollars worth of ***shoes*** annually.

There is a sixth heading entitled ***Cash Advance Items*** that covers all the goods and services the funeral director must pay for at the time of receipt and collect for later, often with an additional fee for doing so. As you might imagine, these are often time-critical expenditures and as such there will not likely be time to shop for them. Included are such items as:

An Honorarium for Clergy
Flowers
Newspaper Notices (obituary or death notice)
Organist
Soloist
Death Certificates (per copy)
Other Funeral Home Charges (parking lot, police escort, etc.)

Air Transportation
Cremation Permit
Acknowledgment/Prayer Cards
Temporary grave marker
Other

It is customary for all these charges to be on a separate summary sheet. Per law, the funeral home is required to inform you what comes under this heading and prevailing costs of each item and, failing a detailed list, provide a 'Good Faith' estimate. They must eventually provide an itemized statement of 'Funeral Goods and Services' purchased and the price for each.

Looking over the above list you will likely find several items you would prefer to handle yourself and, from what I hear from funeral directors, they'd be pleased if you did. These items represent immediate cash paid out by the funeral home plus some extra legwork and phone calls. Still, it's nice to know these things are available, particularly if you've ever tried to locate someone to sing a favorite song, in public, solo, on short notice.

SUMMARY

The short-notice/sudden death funeral is the most challenging to arrange due to time constraints and the decisions that must be made while still in something of an emotional stupor. It is far too easy for a soft-spoken (or guilt-peddling) salesperson to lead you down an expensive path at this time, hence the need for a friend or consultant with a level head to accompany you every step of the way. Make it someone who can say "**NO.**" or at least "**Not yet.**"

More than one sales seminar has used the phrase '***If you can get them crying, you can get them to buying***' and some are not beyond using words and phrases to elicit emotion. Reality must remain in the forefront during negotiations on the arrangements. Stripped to its simplest form, a funeral is merely saying goodbye and disposing of the remains. All else is fluff.

The difference between a crepe and a velvet lining in a casket won't matter to the departed, nor will the bronze, copper, steel, or wood exterior of the casket, nor the handles on a vault, nor the view from the gravesite. What ***will*** matter and be remembered will be the deceased. Set a reasonable budget and insist the funeral director stay within it. Spend more of your time with loved ones and friends and less time sweating the bills.

Remember that time is your enemy in the sudden-death scenario. The temptation to just throw up your hands and let the funeral director make all the decisions for you will be real and also expensive on many levels. Take the time to do it right. Should you encounter anything you need help with, don't hesitate to call a professional consultant or us. Their fees start at about $100 for a phone session, $300 for a home visit and top out at around $750 for someone to literally do the arrangements for you (requires a Special Power of Attorney). Better agencies will guarantee they'll save you much more than that.

II. Arranging the Anticipated Funeral

In the beginning, mankind came to bury its dead not due to religion but in self-defense. There were plenty of predators out there, you see, and the last thing primitive man wanted was to leave bodies around where these creatures could develop a taste for human flesh. With the coming of societal groups, bodies were buried to prevent the spread of diseases such as cholera.

Later, bodies were buried—sometimes with their leg bones broken or the body decapitated—to keep their spirits from wandering. In some areas, particularly in Europe, a wooden or metal spike was driven through the body to 'nail it to the ground' to keep spirits from roaming (***a la Dracula***). To be doubly sure, large stones were placed upon the grave. The tombstone of today is a holdover from this custom.

Despite this long history, no funeral involving someone you know and care about is going to be ***easy*** to arrange. Dr. Elizabeth Kubler-Ross, in her treatise on death and dying, cited the various stages of one's recognition of impending death to include anger, denial, bargaining, depression, and, eventually, acceptance. ***Acceptance*** is the stage when one can actually help shape his or her funeral and should be awaited patiently.

Common sense on the family's behalf will have to reign, of course. The terminally ill are often prone to fanciful mental excursions when contemplating their funerals and this is particularly true in the cases of heavily medicated or demented patients. These excursions will range from a near-total disregard ('***Just toss me into a ditch somewhere!***') to intricate planning that includes engraved invitations and a seating chart!

Somewhere between these extremes lies reality.

Get input on the relevant details such as what clothing they'd prefer, favorite hymns, songs, or poems they'd like read or sung, which clergyman to handle the service, preference in burial or cremation and where. (See the next chapter for a pre-planning guide.) You might also ask if there's anything in particular they'd like mentioned in the obituary or on their headstone. Don't dwell upon the topic too long or the answers will likely get increasingly depressing, but most people ***really would*** like a say in the conduct of their own funerals. After all, they've made decisions all their lives, right?

Speak with the attending physician once the person's condition has defined itself, but don't expect to hear a date-certain such as "***She only has three weeks.***" That is the stuff of movies and television, not real life. Discuss the person's condition with members of the family as far in advance as possible, to let them know the situation and to prepare them for the inevitable.

Now you can get down to actually planning the funeral, in rough form at first and with definition later. Planning will not only save money, it will also free your mind of much of the added stress at a time when you most want to concentrate on the departed and to be with friends and family.

[Editor's Note: As mentioned in the Introduction, many readers will be using this book in an at-need situation and be tempted to skip to the chapter relevant to them at the moment. Hence, there will be repetition of material in each chapter to ensure all the basics are covered. If you are reading cover-to-cover, please pardon this redundancy.]

Last Things First

Given the time to plan, it would benefit you greatly to start at the end and work your way back. Begin with the question, ***where will the remains rest once it's all over?***

If cremation is elected, will the ashes be dispersed somewhere or retained in an urn or other container? If retained, **who** will keep them? Be specific, ill feelings have resulted from simple misunderstandings. Dispersal offers an out when there is a conflict over who will retain the cremains, and at least one company offers nice plaques and framed certificates which may be more comfortably displayed than cremains. Another benefit of cremation is that no decision on ***final*** disposition need be made immediately.

If burial is elected, start at the cemetery. Granted, the marker or monument will be the last decision in this option but this is not an immediate requirement. If your family, church, or community has its own cemetery, which is fairly common in rural areas, this can be quite simple. If you live in an urban setting, however, there's some research to be done if the dying person doesn't already have a plot or mausoleum. If you skipped-over the first section of this book, please go back and read the section on cemeteries for some useful hints on how to save money and avoid problems in the long run.

You should also consider what the future might hold. If it is a spouse you're buying for, do you intend to be buried alongside? What if you re-marry? What if you move? All these are things to consider with a clear head. As mentioned earlier in the book, burial plots are not cheap and there's no sense buying a double plot if only one will be used. Odds are there will be several single plots (and doubles, and family) listed in those classified ads we also mentioned earlier, check them out. After all, it's not as though they're ***used.***

Here are some things to ask on the phone before you visit the cemetery.

*What is the price range of your burial plots?
[Insist upon actual figures, not vague references to '***Complete After-Care Packages'* or the dubious "*It depends ...*"**]

*How do prices vary by geographic location within the cemetery?
[Proximity to walkways or statuary gardens, etc.]

*Do you require a particular type of vault or liner?
[If so, do you provide it in the price of the plot or is it additional? If additional, how much?]

*What is the cost of opening and closing a grave and how does it vary throughout the day and week?

*Does the cemetery require a certain type of monument?
[If so, do you provide it or can I purchase my own from another source? What is the price, required dimensions, installation fees, etc.?]

*What are your visitation policies?
*What is the cemetery's policy on decoration of the graves in terms of flowers, flags, etc.?

As the funeral industry evolves from being primarily family-owned to a corporate entity, you will see more instances where the funeral home, cemetery, crematory, and monument yard are all under one roof (so to speak). This sort of one-stop shopping **could and *should*** allow lower overall prices, but in practice this isn't the case. Instead, it is used as a whip.

If you want a cremation, for instance, there's apt to be one price if the service is handled by the crematory owner's funeral home, and another price if handled by anyone else's. Oddly enough, it is often cheaper when handled elsewhere, but there are likely to be additional fees at the funeral home. Some charge a **Cremation Charge** in addition to the crematory's **Cremation Fee**. This is, in effect, double billing and is commonplace.

The 'Wal-Mart Approach' is on the move in the funeral industry. Don't be surprised to see conglomerate funeral homes and other funeral-related industries move into a moderate sized town and under-sell all the family-owned businesses for a couple of years to drive them out of the business, or at least certain segments of it. Then the prices will go back up.

Be wary of loss leaders such as, ***"We open and close the grave for free."*** or ***"Our limousine service is provided at no cost to the immediate family."*** Expect to pay for each service or expect to ***really pay*** for something else to make up for it.

A cemetery sales person who allowed me to hear part of his spiel cited the following statistic, ***"The cost of a funeral plot doubles every ten years."*** This may be true or he may just have been trying to pitch a multi-unit plot. Price is often dependent upon how many unsold plots remain in the cemetery at the time you purchase. A fairly 'new' cemetery, which is to say one that is less than half-full, will be more likely to have stable and reasonable rates than one 80% occupied or sold, due to the old supply-and-demand maxim. If

Mom and Dad are buried there, the thinking goes, Son and Daughter will be willing to pay more to be buried nearby and the longer they wait to buy, the more they will pay for the privilege.

After you have finished your comparison- shopping by phone, you should visit in person. If there is a cemetery you particularly favor but find it is more costly than another, don't be afraid to mention this fact in dealing with the sales person.

"I like the layout here much better than at Cedar Hill but their price is $500 less for a similar plot and that is closer to my limit. If you will lower the price into my range, we can probably do business."

Yes, ***business.*** At this point you are buying a small piece of real estate and the salesman knows this. If you wait until after the death occurs, you'll be buying peace of mind and the answer to an immediate problem and he'll know that, too. **Don't be afraid to make your own offer and don't be afraid to walk away if they won't deal.** Odds are he'll either follow you out to the parking lot or the phone will be ringing when you get home. The sales person's commission is likely in the 20-45% range on pre-need sales, so there's room for compromise, and you can bet he'll know that as well.

Know in advance that there are at least two prices for everything you see at a cemetery, and in reality there are three. There's the ***At-Need*** price, which is what you'll pay if you wait until the individual is deceased and your need is pressing. At-Need is the highest. Then there's the ***Pre-Need*** price, which applies to purchases in advance of actual use. The pre-need price may be as low as half the at-need rate. There is also ***Absolute*** price, which is what you can get if you take the time to research the other cemeteries and you bargain a bit. This will be the lowest price of all. Now, back to our planning.

At The Cemetery (Services)

In the case of cremation you can skip this part unless you elect to have the ashes interred in the cemetery. Now that we have decided upon where the burial is to take place, let's go over what you want to do there as part of the service. For some, particularly those choosing direct burial, the graveside service is held in lieu of a formal funeral, perhaps with a memorial service held later.

If the actual funeral service is held elsewhere, the cemetery portion may be attended by just family or open to all. The finality of the deceased actually going into the ground tends to heighten emotions, so some prefer limiting the graveside portion to just family. Closing the grave can be particularly traumatic to children, so please read the section regarding children and funerals later in this chapter.

Some elect to have a final prayer while the casket sits on its device over the grave, then depart while it is enclosed in the vault, sealed, and the grave filled. They return later to situate floral acknowledgments, take photographs and so forth. Others prefer the ancient custom of tossing in a handful of soil after the casket is in the grave. Again, it is your choice, but be sure to remember that graveside services are particularly hard on those who must get around with walkers or wheelchairs, so have plenty of assistance available.

If you elect a graveside funeral service everything will happen here. You will need chairs, a tent (weather dependant), a pulpit or rostrum for the minister (though he or the funeral home may provide this), and perhaps sound equipment if there is to be a large crowd. Whether or not you need a tent will depend upon the weather, but consider this; less than one day in four (on average) is a good day for an outdoor service of any duration. During the extremes of summer and winter the odds are even worse.

For veterans, the graveside portion of the funeral is particularly poignant. The rifle salute followed by a bugler playing Taps (particularly if there is another bugler at a distance echoing it) and concluding with the formal folding and presentation of the flag is moving regardless of what your stand on military service may be. It is an honor earned for a service rendered to our country. See Appendix A for information on arranging these services as well as other entitlements that may accrue to survivors.

There is often an uneasy moment just after the graveside service. The formal part of the ceremony is largely over, yet often people are reluctant to leave and uncertain what protocol to follow if they stay. One should endeavor to offer a final condolence to the family before departing, but not in a constant parade like the receiving line at a banquet. At the end of the service the minister can either issue an invitation to a reception later, or wish everyone a safe drive home, as the family wishes. This lets attendees know the ceremony is completed and frees them to go their separate ways (they'll have a chance to talk later, after all). Either way, it's better than standing around wondering what to do next.

Getting There

How will you get to the cemetery? Most funeral homes now have limousines available, at a charge, for the immediate family. Additional limos are often available (through the funeral home) at a slightly inflated rental rate or you can hire them directly from a limo company. A cost-saving option here would be renting an upscale automobile from a rental agency or car dealership and having a relative drive. Either way, you'll need to decide who rides with whom in advance so no one is left behind and those needing support (due to infirm health, difficulty in getting around, or emotionally overcome) will have it.

Another thing to consider is the police escort. The funeral director generally arranges this and there may be a fee. If you know someone in local or state law enforcement you can inquire about it yourself, or just phone the nearest precinct or sheriff's office. Often such services are provided to taxpayers at no charge, though some units (such as State Troopers) may have restrictions on this. Make certain everyone knows that the vehicles carrying the immediate family and those requiring assistance will have priority on parking spaces nearest the site.

Leaving the Chapel

It is not uncommon for family, friends, and neighbors to file past the deceased for a final viewing following the funeral service. Since this will likely be the last time the casket is opened, the family may want to remain for a few minutes to say their farewells before departing the chapel or church.

Between the time the family exits the chapel and the funeral procession is ready to transit to the gravesite, the funeral director's staff has some things to do. First, they must close and seal the casket then there will be floral arrangements to pack into a van for the trip. They may want to depart ahead of the family to ensure everything is in readiness at the cemetery when family and guests arrive. Coordinate this with the funeral director.

Feel free to join friends and family outside or in the lobby during this time and ask the funeral director to let you know when to start for the limousine or your automobile. If pallbearers are used, their exit from the chapel with the casket will be the signal. Without an understanding on this, you'll likely end up with some restive guests sitting in their cars for a long time or left behind.

You've already decided who will ride with whom, who will need assistance and each car's position behind the hearse and police cruiser. If you've decided you'd be more comfortable having only immediate family at the cemetery, by all means have either the minister or the funeral director announce this prior to the service beginning so there'll be no misunderstanding. He can include it in a general "Thank you for coming out" statement so no one will be slighted, or even cite scarcity of seating or parking (as at some mausoleums) as a regrettable reason for having to limit participation to just the family.

The Funeral Service

When one hears the word ***funeral***, the ceremony is what comes to mind. Over the years the funeral industry's main players have changed their title from ***undertaker***, to ***mortician***, to the current ***funeral***

director. This is far more accurate than the previous titles since they do indeed ***direct***.

Some funeral homes have three or more services per day. Don't be stunned if the staff allots a certain block of time for your service, and don't be surprised to see the funeral director prompting the minister to speed things up if he gets windy. It's a running joke on the funeral industry that they shoo one family out of the chapel just in time for the next family to enter. If there are multiple services to be held in the same chapel, the deceased may be rolled in and out like a scenery change in the theater.

This is what funerals have become, but more and more families are taking back control and having the ceremony **they** want. The old saying "*It's **your** funeral!*" really applies here; decide what you want and have the establishment adhere to your wishes.

As was the case in the previous chapter, I'll make no attempt here to go through the diversity of funeral customs among the world's two thousand-plus religions and hundreds of cultures. If you think of something special that you'd like, odds are it has been done before. Get with your family, your minister, priest, rabbi, etc. and, most importantly, the 'Guest of Honor' while there's time, to decide what the ceremony will be.

A good way to plan this is to allot a time period for the whole ceremony and work within it. Say you select thirty minutes as a likely span for the entire affair. If there's to be three hymns sung, at a little over three minutes each, there's ten minutes accounted for. Give the minister five to ten minutes, another two or three minutes for prayers or communal reading of scriptures and perhaps five to seven minutes for an eulogy. Now arrange these segments to suit you.

It's that simple? Of course not! Well, not often anyway. Some religions have a prescribed funeral ceremony that can go on long enough to require a meal! Some will have several friends and family members get up to say a few words. Others may prefer more hymns, extra prayers, a soloist or choir, communion, an instrumental number with silent introspection, reading of a poem, and a range of other options. **The point is, make the ceremony your own or, better yet, make it what the *deceased* wanted.**

There is no one ***right*** way to remember a deceased family member. Just keep in mind that, no matter what the service entails, it is for the living.

Children and Funerals

There's no hard-and-fast rule on how young is ***too*** young to attend a funeral, but there's a wealth of touchy-feely advice out there about how to deal with kids and death. I'll leave this to the professionals, but would recommend one source of enlightenment.

Family Communications publishes a series of booklets on the subject (the ***Let's Talk About It*** series), as well as videotapes. The booklet ***Talking With Young Children About Death*** is quite well done as is the video ***Mister Rogers Talks About Living and Dying***. This video, which is narrated by the late Fred Rogers, touches upon many of children's concerns. It may be available at your local library, via a hospice center, or even through some of the more-progressive funeral homes. You can also call Family Communications, Inc., at (412) 687-2990.

Should children attend the funeral or not?

It's **your** call. One of the more memorable funeral evolutions I ever attended occurred when I was living in southern California. A neighbor died suddenly (cerebral hemorrhage) and, as spread-out as San Diego County is, the funeral service and the burial were to be miles apart. This posed a not-so-unique problem for all of us with small children, but the way the family addressed this problem was sheer genius.

For about $200, they arranged sitters, a clown, and pony rides at a community center. Parents dropped-off their darlings, went on to the services and reclaimed them two hours later. The kids enjoyed themselves immensely and whining or trips to the bathroom did not disrupt the services. In short, it was a positive experience all-around.

I'm not saying a funeral should be a cause for celebration among the younger generation, just that taking some action (identify a nearby care center, for instance, and let parents know) is preferable to hoping for the best or risk hurting someone's feelings by declaring children unwelcome. A little forethought, plus a little brainstorming with your friends, can help allay any problems children might present. Children are easily distracted outdoors, so you might want to exclude them from graveside services.

The Prelude

Preceding the actual funeral service there are hours, or in some cases days, during which friends and family will stop by to pay their respects, visit with other mourners, and view the deceased. This is, of course, assuming you've elected to have the deceased available for viewing. The viewing portion of most funerals is equal parts verification and curiosity. On the one hand it provides a verification that the guest of honor has indeed passed away.

Izzy: *"Big John Gilwort is dead."*

Lizzy: *"I'll believe it when I see it!"*

It also tends to draw in friends and relatives well in advance of the actual funeral service. This allows time for even the more distant relatives to provide their opinions (if desired) on the arrangements to come. Some will come out of curiosity *("Wonder what his son has been up to since we graduated reform school?")* and some will come to speak with the family if a prior commitment prevents them from attending the formal service. Funerals make great reunions, and some will come for no lesser reason.

Since we are living longer these days, it is becoming increasingly common for the aged and infirm to request there NOT be a viewing due to the wasting effects of a long illness. As with the case of a severe trauma-related death (for example an automobile accident), the family may wish a portrait or photograph to be placed upon the closed casket instead of having a direct viewing. This is perfectly acceptable and halts the ***"Don't he look natural?"*** comments I've always found rather bizarre.

In fact, several studies show a trend toward having a direct burial or cremation with a modest ceremony held later at a church, chapel, the graveside or in the home. This scenario, while gaining popularity with the general public who is tired of inflated prices and prolonged ordeals, is not supported by the funeral industry for obvious reasons; it would cut funeral and burial costs by up to 80%!

Consider what would NOT be required in this case:

*Embalming
*Additional transportation fees
*Most funeral home staff and facilities charges
*Cosmetic and hair-dressing charges
*Chapel rental
*Viewing fees
*Common Areas charges
*Parking lot fees
*Professional Service Fees
*Forwarding and Receiving of remains
*Other fees and charges

For now, however, it is somewhat expected that as many as half of all funerals will involve the usual several days of viewing and visitation. In theory this allows distant friends and relatives time to travel. In practice it drives the economics of funerals sky high and adds to the emotional burden on the grieving family by extending things for several days, during which they will have to recount everything concerning the deceased's demise numerous times.

Viewing periods should be attended by at least one member of the deceased's family and should be scheduled for the convenience of those wishing to pay their respects. During the week this means a period in the late afternoon or evening to accommodate work schedules. You may want an optional period during the mid-morning or early afternoon for those who have children in school, wish to visit during their lunch hour, or work odd hours.

Someone in the family should put visitors at ease during these visits—there will be plenty of time for open mourning at the funeral. I say this with full realization that there will be those who think otherwise, that every moment involved should be solely dedicated to mourning the deceased with no conversation directed elsewhere. In practice, this flies in the face of human nature.

Old friends and relatives one hasn't seen in a long time will be dropping by. They will want to extend their conversations beyond the passing of the deceased and nothing could be more natural. The family will value some distraction and a visit from an old friend, replete with bringing one another up-to-date on their lives, telling stories and reminiscing about old times, even exchanging jokes, is time well-spent. It is an integral part of the healing process. For this reason whatever the charge for common areas such as a kitchen, coffee lounge, or parlor, it is well worth it.

Enjoying a moment or two shows respect for life, not disrespect for the dead.

Having another relative on the scene to relieve the widow or widower so that they may adjourn to the parlor/kitchen to be with these relatives and friends in less-emotional surroundings is paramount. Speaking in the hushed tones one hears in a chapel is hard on the throat so do take a break to 'wet your whistle' now and then.

Another suggestion is to station a relative near the sign-in book (register) to get the name of each visitor and introduce him or her to the next-of-kin. This is particularly important with the elderly who don't need the added stress of playing ***Guess Who I Am*?** with long-unseen visitors and relatives repeatedly while in mourning.

There is another good reason to hold the number of viewing periods to a minimum. They take so much out of the survivors that, by the time the actual funeral ceremony is held, they are often too fatigued to feel much of anything beyond relief. See to it the closest family members and the more emotional friends get adequate rest and time away from the viewing area.

A word about the kitchen; ***don't try to feed the world***! There are many caterers who would be more than happy to put on most any sort of spread you will pay for, but it is neither necessary nor expected. For the viewing periods, be it at a funeral home chapel, a church annex or in your own home, coffee and perhaps some light snacks is plenty.

In many areas of the country it is customary for friends, neighbors and relatives to bring offerings of food and these are very well received along with tea and/or coffee. If you'd like a wake before or perhaps a reception following the services, by all means go ahead, but keep the prelude fare reasonable.

As to modes of behavior and etiquette in the viewing area or at the funeral service itself, there really are no guidelines. Be strong or stricken but be yourself.

Selecting a Funeral Home

As explained earlier, this should be done prior to having the body moved. Since you'll have adequate time to do some comparison-shopping you'll stand a better chance of holding funeral expenses to a reasonable level. The initial criteria for selecting a funeral home will likely be equal parts tradition, reputation, and research. Few funeral homes just spring up like toadstools overnight and it is rare for them to last but a single generation, so finding someone with personal experience dealing with each funeral home should not be hard. Ask around.

As a rule funeral homes are local concerns, which is to say they are located in—and market to—a specific area. This local focus is moot when considering which home to handle the service, because some count on the community's loyalty rather than competitive pricing. Call around outside your neighborhood and bear in mind that the more extensive the facade and the more numerous the staff, the higher charges will likely be to cover excess overhead.

Call and request price lists on services and funeral goods, be it caskets and vaults or cremains urns. By the way, those ornate little boxes and vases for storing ashes can run into the THOUSANDS OF DOLLARS! Don't go for the ***"Well, we can store about half of your grandma in this unit, for about seven hundred dollars, or we can put all of her in this one for just three hundred more."*** ploy. You can provide your own container, be it a paper sack, a Tupperware bowl, or a rare Ming vase, so don't be swayed by a sales pitch for something designed with this purpose in mind.

What we're talking about with ***cremains*** is merely the pulverized remains of the more-compact bones, a substance somewhere between sand and kitty litter in consistency. Some of the most beautiful containers I've seen, by the way, were designed as Cigar Humidors. I have seen mahogany boxes sold as a cremains urn for over $900 at a funeral home and the ***very same box sold as a cigar humidor for $79.95 at a tobacco shop!***

Use your imagination and, while you're looking, have the cremains stored in a ***minimal container***, which is a plastic box costing $10-$25 and supplied by the crematory. Also, forget the 'scattering urns', if you're going to scatter do it from the plastic box or the plastic bag inside it.

I recently learned of an interesting example of this very thing. My sister had returned to college to complete an advanced nursing degree and had a classmate who was pursuing a second career. The classmate had been a flight attendant and her late husband a pilot and they had traveled much of the world together.

Per his wishes, she kept his ashes and each time she or a friend traveled to somewhere her husband had never been, along went a pinch of his ashes for distribution. When my sister asked the lady exactly where her late husband's cremains were at present, she said they were in a small plastic box serving as a bookend for her nursing books. When Sis informed the widow she was going to the Cayman Islands on vacation and asked if she'd like her to take along a 'Pinch of Fred', the widow replied, "Thank you but no, he’s been there."

I find this attitude refreshing, but the funeral industry wouldn't care much for it since very little in the way of goods or services are involved. This goes back to the point I made about making everything about the service and disposal of remains what the **deceased** would want and hang what is customary! A funeral is a social event and the disposition of the remains a personal decision. This is why getting the ‘guest of honor’s’ input is so vital, both for his or her satisfaction and your peace of mind.

Once you have the rudimentary price information in-hand, make a tour of the various funeral homes. **Expect some pressure to put your name on a dotted line or at least verbally agree to a contract for services**. Resist and take your friend along to be the dissenting voice, should you need one. Having the

'Guest of Honor' still alive and furnishing a big part of the decision-making process, is an automatic ***out*** should you encounter pressure; ***"I'll need to bounce this off Aunt Trudy and see what she prefers."***

Let me caution you again about your mode of dress when visiting these establishments. The funeral director and his sales force are masters at summing-up economic potential at a glance. If you arrive dressed to the nines, wearing a Rolex and upscale jewelry, you can bet you won't be shown anything but top-of-the-line caskets, vaults, and service packages.

Not that you should show-up wearing sackcloth and ashes, of course, but bear in mind that all the mood-lighting, velvet drapes, soft carpets and smooth voices are designed to create an atmosphere of profound respectability. It often comes at a price. Just be aware that those who pay $700 for a respectable casket will get the same atmosphere as those who mortgage their futures for a swank bronze number.

Check such pedestrian things as available parking, lounge areas, cleanliness and attitude of the staff you encounter. If they yank you in off the porch, you might want to look elsewhere. Most will be considerate and admire you taking the initiative to plan ahead. Some may even suggest ways of holding expenses down, if you just ask. They aren't all ogres.

Let them know up-front that you have discussed the required services at-length with the 'Guest of Honor' and that your needs will be specific, right down to the make and model of the vault. This lets them know you'll not be easily swayed nor led along more expensive paths, and that you have at least a nodding acquaintance with the arrangement process.

If nothing else, this book should give you a familiarity with the terminology used in the funeral industry and this alone will set you apart from the usual customer. A hint from a long-time consumer advocate is to check the toilet paper in the restrooms. If it's plush, they care about families, if it's a cheap industrial single-ply that tears off one square at a time, move on! They're more interested in profits than service.

THE OBITUARY

How would the deceased like his or her name to appear in print? ***Allouitious Cumquat Barkolounger*** might prefer he be listed as ***Al Barkolounger*** in his obituary, to cite a rather extreme example. It bears discussion and so does how they'd like the engraving on the headstone to read. Address this topic early since it will be important, both in the immediate future and—since the monument will be all that remains visible after the funeral—***forever***.

An example not quite so far-fetched involves a gentleman who for at least four decades I'm aware of, sold fresh produce at a roadside stand. Year-round he would be out there offering whatever was in-season and helping customers choose wisely from his bins. Then, he just disappeared.

Everyone wondered why and it finally got around that he had passed away, but it was weeks after the funeral before any of his customers knew he'd died. In addition to the sadness of his departure, there was that awful feeling many of us had neglected to honor this old casual friend.

Why? Because the man had been known forever as ***Red* Fuller** of ***Red's Fresh Produce,*** and in his obituary he was "Harry W. Fuller, Jr., a local merchant." Could

Harry W. 'Red' Fuller, Jr., local fresh produce merchant have alerted more of his friends and customers? Probably. Make certain you word any death notice or obituary in such a way that friends and acquaintances will know who has died.

ASK!

There are a host of other things to consider in the obituary and, if at all possible, the person about whom it is written should have the final edit. Will the cause of death be cited? It varies with the newspaper and the family's wishes, unless you take the initiative to state one way or the other in advance.

Often something generic such as " ... following an extended illness." will suffice without getting into the particulars. This is particularly important in the case of suicide, homicide, some types of accidental death (would you want the world to know you bent down to tie your shoe and got your tie caught in an escalator?) and death from some diseases.

How will survivors be listed? **"*She is survived by her husband, William Floyd Marshall*"**, or **"*Survivors include her husband of thirty-six years, William Floyd Marshall, and two daughters: Melany Grant of Springfield and Betty Marshall of Great Falls, along with four grandchildren.*"** Either way is acceptable, but some guidelines would assist whoever must sit down and draft the thing.

A thorny problem has developed over the past three decades; **how does one list an ex-husband or ex-wife among the survivors?** Some will merely say, **don't**! For others, particularly those who had children with this person or remained relatively close after divorce, inclusion of the ***Ex-*** seems natural enough. Again, ask.

Additional information on writing a death notice and obituary can be found on the data sheet that we'll be coming to later in the planning stage. For now you need to decide what things about the deceased bear mentioning in the obituary. Retired teacher? Vietnam veteran? Avid golfer? Include the things that will help define the person and to clarify who has passed on. Remember the fresh produce guy?

Notification of Friends and Family

Okay, you'll need a list. A roster, if you will. The more complete and current the list, the easier this particular task will be. In the next section you'll find such a list and I encourage you to fill it out immediately. Include work, cell and home phone numbers, beeper (pager) numbers, electronic mail (e-mail) addresses and street addresses.

Gather them into geographic headings with someone you can trust at the head of each of these geographic lists. When the time comes have the person at the head of each list to phone everyone below them. You can hand them a copy, fax it, or read it over the phone, but get it to them. This ***Call Tree*** will buy you time for the other tasks we addressed earlier.

In the case of the anticipated death the news will be easier to accept on the other end, providing everyone has been made aware of the deceased's condition beforehand. For the infirm and truly close relatives, you might want to notify them indirectly (via another relative or friend) so someone can be with them for support when they learn of the death. This is a particular consideration for those with significant medical histories.

Selecting Your Friend, Co-planner or Shopping Partner

In the first section of this book we cited the First Rule; ***Don't go alone!*** Okay, who will it be? It should be someone whose judgment you trust, someone with spine enough to say '***No***!' or at least '***Not yet***.', someone you can reach in an instant and remain close to for several days. That narrows it down considerably, doesn't it? For now we'll consider someone other than a professional consultant.

Select a couple of potential assistants, prioritize them and never let them know who was your first choice. Ideally you'll want someone a bit removed from the deceased, for objectivity, and someone who has been through the funeral arrangement process within the past few years, for experience. Beyond this, you'll want a friend. Make your best picks and let them help when the time comes. As you will realize by now, there are a lot of decisions to make and lots of things to remember, so two minds are better than one. This also gives you someone to carry the tissues.

Payment Options

No matter what option you elect you will at some point realize you have to pay for it. This is often the last consideration, coming as it does at the end of the arrangement visit, and for many the first inkling of the true costs involved. The bill may come as a shock, particularly to those who may have difficulty coming up with the total sum. The fact is that no part of the arrangement will go forward until the establishment is satisfied you ***can*** and ***will*** pay the bill in full. If the body has already been collected it may be held in storage until a suitable payment method is found. Fortunately, there are numerous options available and we'll address these in some detail.

Cash

Yes, cash is still accepted by all funeral-related businesses. If you have that much cash on hand you probably don't need this book.

Credit Card

A few years ago this would have seemed an unusual choice. Given the increased limits and decreased interest rates here in the early years of the new millennium, however, it can be a valid choice. If you find yourself needing to pay the bill on installments, you'll likely find the funeral establishment charges an industry-wide average of 1.5% per MONTH on any unpaid balance. Contrast this with a credit card with, say, a 7.9% interest rate per YEAR (albeit compounded daily) and you'll realize a major savings in interest and probably lower monthly payments.

Viatical Settlements

This is a rather new wrinkle brought about largely by the AIDS crisis of the 1980s. What this amounts to is cash received for ***assigning*** all or a portion of a life insurance policy. If you're looking to buy in advance and take advantage of 'pre-need' prices, you can 'sell' the future proceeds of a life insurance policy in force on the terminal patient or on anyone else who is willing. The proceeds will be discounted, of course. If the insured is terminal with a prognosis of dying within, say, the next six months, you might receive as much as 90% of the amount assigned. If the prognosis is for death within the next year, the rate might drop to 80% and so on.

Viatical sales are short-term investments on the buyer's side and the answer to short-term financial problems on the seller's. Using the example above, a man diagnosed with terminal, inoperable, lung cancer with a prognosis of death within the next three months could assign $10,000 of his $50,000 life insurance policy and receive $9,000 within days. With this money he could buy funeral goods and services at pre-need prices and perhaps save $3,000 or more, plus save his family a lot of stress. At death his beneficiary would receive the remaining $40,000 death benefit from the policy.

To cite another example, let's say this same man has no life insurance in force but his wife has a $50,000 policy. She can assign $12,000 of the future proceeds of her policy and, depending on her health and actuary tables for her age, receive as much as $9,000.

In most cases the entity buying the assignment will assume payment of premiums to ensure the policy remains in force. The projected cost of these premiums will be factored into the discount rate and settlement amount.

Whole Life Insurance

Whole Life or Participating Life or whatever it goes by when you read this is essentially an overpriced term policy with part of the overcharge invested to grow 'cash value'. One is led to believe that if he has a $50,000 whole life policy and the cash value (the amount you can withdraw, albeit as a LOAN against the death benefit) after 20 years of premiums is $35,000, his beneficiary has $85,000 coming at the death of the policyholder. WRONG! The typical language used when you ask about this is "***The cash value at time of death is included in the death benefit.***"

What they mean is, no matter what the cash value you'll never receive more than the face value … the $35,000 you have accrued goes to help the insurance company pay your $50,000. Where its name is fitting is that you can elect, once you have cash value built up, to take paid-up insurance in the amount of that cash value and it will remain in force your ***whole life***. For older persons who have outlived the term insurance ceilings, this can be a godsend.

> **Example:** *John has died without any insurance or prepayment of funeral expenses. Mary has a $50,000 whole life policy she's had for 15 years and it has accrued a cash value of $12,000. Mary can, at her option, withdraw $8,000 of the cash value to pay for John's funeral expenses. This may be an answer to the short-term financial crunch, but she should be aware of what she is doing.*

The insurance company will count the withdrawal as a LOAN and charge her interest on the $8,000 either in the form of increased premiums (if she elects) or by debiting her remaining cash value each month to cover the interest until the 'loan' is repaid in full. Some may even reduce her death benefit by the difference between the loan ($8,000) and the remaining cash value ($4,000) should she die before repaying the balance.

Something to consider in this case is the cost of keeping this policy in force versus its value on the viatical market. If Mary is elderly or in frail health, she might well be ahead of the game to assign the entire policy to a viatical settlement company for cash and let THEM pay the remaining premiums. This is where you need to consult a family lawyer, a financial planner, or a member of the Society of Certified Senior Advisors (CSAs) for advice.

Insurance Benefit Assignment

This is the most common form of payment and bears a word of caution. In its simplest form, the family shows up for the arrangement visit with the deceased's insurance policy or policies. Among the first items the staff person will ask is "***How many certified copies of the Death Certificate will you need?***" He may go on to explain you'll need one for Social Security, one for the Bureau of Vital Statistics, etc., but the important thing is you'll need one for each insurance policy in force at the time of death. If you recount the number of policies in front of him you're giving a good indication of how much you have to spend on the FUNERAL.

If there are multiple policies it's good to keep this information to yourself until ***after*** the bill is totaled. Then you can say, "You know? I'm not sure about that number of certified copies of the death certificate. To be safe, let's get several."

Some in the funeral industry have come to look upon ***life insurance*** as ***burial insurance,*** in other words as ***theirs***. We have helped foster this opinion by saying, "I have enough insurance to put me away." Or, "Aunt Tilly left a $10,000 life insurance policy so we felt honor-bound to spend it all on the funeral." Remember the example cited earlier of the widow with her husband's $12,000 policy who walked out with a funeral costing $12,000 to the penny? This is a classic example of how some establishments will find a way to soak up an entire policy if given the chance. So, how do you avoid this?

You pay with an insurance policy by ***assigning*** enough of its benefits to cover the bill. No more. If you have a policy with $25,000 in benefits and the funeral bill comes to $4300 (after some clever decisions, the national average in 2003 was about $6100 just for the funeral home portion) you may be asked to assign the entire policy. The understanding is that the funeral home will ***take care of this for you*** then rebate the remainder. DON'T!

Assign only enough to cover the bill plus a few hundred extra to cover 'out of pocket' expenditures the funeral home will pay on your behalf. You may well need funds in the near future to cover other things and don't want to have all the insurance benefits tied up with one assignment. If the funeral home deposits the proceeds into its trust account pending release of the remainder to you, it is drawing interest and has little incentive to return your balance quickly. Guard your resources carefully and don't let emotion drive you to decisions that will cause you financial problems down the road.

Here's a tip that might pay dividends; look for insurance that doesn't come with a policy. Some fraternal and veteran's organizations give their members a small insurance policy as part of their membership. Credit cards, particularly the upscale Gold & Platinum accounts, sometimes include accidental death benefits, travel insurance, etc.

Indigent Burial

We receive several calls each week asking for funds for funerals. We are not in this end of the business, but for those who find themselves short of funds there are some alternatives.

Veterans, in some circumstances, are entitled to funds from the U.S. Government via the VA. The ***Veteran's Cremation & Burial Society*** offers a network of providers, many of them veterans themselves, that offers funeral services at rates as much as 40% lower than the national average. Membership currently costs $35, they have a financing program for those who need it, and you can contact them by phone at 800-467-7850 or on the Internet at ***www.veteransfuneralcare.com***

Churches and Charities can sometimes help. Contact your minister, priest, rabbi, etc. and ask what is available in the way of assistance. Catholic Charities and Jewish Family Services are likely sources and you do not have to be Catholic or Jewish to apply. Just be aware their funds may be limited.

Most states and many municipalities have funds for indigent burial (average between $500 and $1500 nationally). Contact your local Social Services and ask. There may be funds available through Medicare in some instances, though these funds are limited and rare by the end of the fiscal year.

Burial Insurance, Pre-purchase and Prepayment Plans

Should you decide to take the initiative and insure, pre-pay, or pre-purchase all or part of your funeral goods and services, proceed with caution! There may be money to be saved—perhaps the difference between paying for a product/service today and buying it with inflation later. This assumes the funeral establishment will honor this agreement and that the program is 'portable' should you die in another city or state. There are several ways to go about this, but you should be aware that it is a rare prepaid funeral that doesn't require additional outlays of several hundred to several thousands of dollars from the family.

Burial Insurance

There is a booming burial insurance industry out there that bears some defining. First off, consider what insurance ***really is*** and how they stay in business. In essence, it is betting against the odds of the policy being collected upon by sharing the risk among many. It can be as simple as letting you pick a benefit figure, say the cost of a complete funeral at today's prices, and issuing you a term life insurance policy to cover that amount with the funeral home as beneficiary. This will work, providing you are insurable, pay the premiums promptly and that you take into account the rather steep inflation of funeral costs over the years (about 10% per year).

You've no doubt seen some of these programs offered on TV 'Infomercials' or flyers included with your Sunday newspapers. Most are legitimate, in so far as they don't violate the tenets of any laws, but several go to great lengths to violate the spirit of these laws.

Let's take a 'for instance':

> *"The DELUXE GOLD PLAN will provide immediate funds for your funeral, up to and including $10,000! AND, it'll do this for less than you normally spend on postage stamps each month. No physical examination required, coverage available from eight-to-eighty! No salesman will call so just phone for FREE information right this very instant! You owe it to your family."*

Now let's take that little spiel apart and see what you're ***really*** buying;

"*... immediate funds for your funeral...*" Maybe, depends upon your definition of ***immediate***. For some companies this can mean as much as three months after the death of the insured because they are selling a repackaged product. You pay them premiums at an inflated rate, they pay another company premiums at a lower rate and this extra layer of bureaucracy can build in delays. Rest assured, you'd not collect before ***they do*** and you may pay interest each month on any unpaid balances.

"*... up to and including $10,000!*" For age eight, definitely. For age eighty? Expect a truly monstrous premium or a lower benefit.

" *... for less than you normally spend on postage stamps each month!*" A ridiculous claim, how do they know how much you spend on postage? But, taking that example, say they contend the average family buys two books of stamps per month, that's $14.80 (as of

2004, or 2 X $7.40 per book of 20) for a $10,000 policy assuming full coverage. That amounts to $17.76 per year per $1,000 of policy, which, by the time they put in the terms limiting pay-out the first couple or three years, is no bargain! Ask your insurance agent.

"***No physical examination required, . . .***" No, but you can bet there will be medical history questions and that they will assign you to a risk group to determine premiums.

"***... coverage available from eight-to-eighty.***" You bet, and for the right premium you can get someone to cover you *after* you're dead! Anything that sounds too good to be true, is.

"***No salesman will call.***" No, but a ***helpful administrative assistant*** will be sure to give you a jingle just to make sure you received the information and offer you further insights into the program. If no salesman is going to call, why do they ask for your phone number?

"***You owe it to your family.***" Actually, you owe it to your family, and yourself, to not be taken-in by one of these doom-and-gloom rip-offs.

These Burial Insurance (or ***Final Expense***) plans are generally just repackaging of an existing product, from another company, at a huge mark-up. In other words, they sell you ***guaranteed renewable term*** insurance, which they buy through another company at the usual rates, charge you a higher rate, and name themselves as the beneficiary. Should you die while covered, they'll collect from ***their*** insurance company, pocket the excess premiums you were charged AND possibly the difference between the policy amount and the funeral costs. In essence, you are overpaying for a product your own insurance broker could likely set up for you at a more reasonable price. Also, some of these companies have a nasty habit of disappearing every few years to resurface under another name.

Yes, I am aware that some policies claim they'll cover anyone of any age, possibly without a physical and often have big-name entertainment personalities pitching them on TV. Read the fine print! In many cases **if you are over age 80 (as an example), no matter how long the policy is in force and even if you pay your premiums religiously, the total benefit you'll receive is equal to the amount of premiums you paid during the FIRST TWO OR THREE YEARS, plus 10%**. This being the case, one would likely be better off with a Totten Trust, which we'll cover shortly.

In-House Prepayment Plans

Another way to pay is what I refer to as Burial ***Assurance***, which is to say having everything paid for in advance so the effects of inflation are reduced. Some casket companies offer this and it is a sound program in most respects. You can select a casket and vault, pay for them now, and be done with it. At the time of your death either the model selected or the nearest newer model of 'equal or superior value' will be delivered. The savings realized are equal to the inflation between the time you buy and the time you die. Naturally, this option has its problems.

Questions you should ask of any pre-payment or pre-purchase program include;

*What if I move? Are the benefits transferable?
*What if the funeral home goes out of business before I die, will I receive a refund? And if so, will it include interest?
*What if my accrued benefits are more than the funeral package selected, who will receive the excess funds?

You also want to make certain a photograph of the model(s) casket you select is included with your contract or receipt. Just '***One Gray Metal Casket***' won't do, since they run from $400-$10,000 and come in hundreds of variants. A specified model number, style of interior, and any extras should be specified, along with the photo brochure.

There are some rather unscrupulous organizations who will tell you that a pre-paid funeral (in some states) is a way to ***buy-down*** one's assets to qualify for state-sponsored (or Medicaid/Medicare) nursing home benefits and reap a tax-free profit in the process. They will say you can pre-pay an outrageous figure, let's say $50,000, thereby lowering the patient's net worth to the point his or her nursing home bills are covered by federal or state programs. Then when the patient dies, a less expensive funeral arrangement can be selected with the beneficiary receiving the difference as a tax-free windfall.

There are several things wrong with the above scenario. First, it is ethically wrong and abuses an otherwise responsible option. Second, it amounts to ***fraud*** and could have some serious repercussions for all involved. Third, it implies that the funeral home making the offer is prone to dishonest and immoral practices. If this is the case, they'll be just as likely to defraud you as the government! **Run from anyone or any establishment making such an offer and find someone you can trust**. Which leads us nicely into the next topic, trusts.

Trusts

Another prepayment program is the Totten Trust. This is sort of a savings plan that is controlled by the consumer. He or she opens the account, deposits a sum of money equal to the cost of the funeral service and wares selected (or pays into it periodically) and can close the account at any time. These deposits are held as passbook savings, certificates of deposit, or money market funds, with the earnings helping defray inflation. A lawyer is often needed to set one of these up, but some funeral homes work directly with banks to establish these trusts. Unlike other forms, **Totten Trusts are available in every state.**

A major benefit of the Totten Trust is that any funds remaining after funeral services are paid to survivors. Also, if you elect to cancel the trust, all principal and interest are returned. This is not necessarily the case with other popular trusts such as the California Master Trust, Golden Rule, NFDA, and NSM Trusts, which may be paid to the funeral director and an administrative fee retained in the event of cancellation. **Funeral home programs generally allow the funeral home to pocket interest on their trust accounts. Have your lawyer check any contract BEFORE you sign it.**

Other Considerations

What if you die before the entire amount bargained for is paid? In the case of a CD-based program, your family will pay the difference between what is in the account, including accrued interest, and the actual cost of the funeral. If an insurance-based program (which has its interest rate generally tied to the Gross National Product or the Consumer Price Index for earnings), the cost is paid in full. Oh, and you'll want a program wherein earnings are based upon the CPI since historically it grows faster than the GNP.

These programs are regulated by the states and vary widely. In some states as little as 60% of the amount you pay into a funeral home directed program is required to be placed in the interest-bearing trust account with the rest available for whatever use the home wishes. Other states vary up to 90-100% and this can make a real difference in the end.

Know what you're getting and don't let any soft-voiced, ***"I only have your best interests at heart."*** sales person steer you into anything—if he wasn't making good money on it he wouldn't be trying to sell it!

Overview of Prepayment Plans

Okay, let's address the reputation of such programs as were just outlined. There have been numerous unfavorable articles in the press and on TV about fraudulent and deceptive practices concerning burial insurance and prepayment programs. Some of these programs have simply folded their tents and stole off into the night, taking their investors' money with them. Others have misdirected funds into expanding their businesses, only to go bankrupt leaving their unwitting ***investors*** unprotected. **These are rare**.

An annual figure often cited as the amount ***missing or unaccounted for*** among prepayment plans nationwide is $50 Million. On the surface that seems like a lot of money, but consider the BILLIONS of dollars that are paid 'as advertised' by these programs and it is minuscule. **Probably 99% of all prepayment (*not* insurance) programs out there are legitimate and worth investigating**, and the Federal Trade Commission is working to weed-out the one percent that isn't. Let your representatives in Congress know it's important to you and they'll likely take action to make the funeral industry even more open with their operations than they've been in the past.

Summary

That should cover arranging the anticipated death funeral. Granted, there's much that is similar to the sudden death funeral, but this is to be expected when the end-result is the same. There's a rule I've developed in theory that you can prove or disprove in practice; **two hours of effort, two weeks in advance can save you two thousand dollars**. Perhaps more. Let me know how you make out.

The next chapter goes hand in hand with what we've just covered, only with a more personal and interactive approach. This personal planning is only valuable for those who realize they will one day perish. Approach it with the realization that every minute spent on it will likely prevent hours of sleepless uncertainty on behalf of your loved ones when your time comes.

Having everything thought out and committed to record is among the most loving gifts you can leave your family.

III. Pre-Planning a Funeral Service

Now we know what goes into a funeral arrangement and we know how to shop for the best price for quality goods and services. It is logical that we now take pen in hand and attack the problem in advance on our own or a loved-one's behalf. To be even more logical, I suggest you use a **pencil**. All things are subject to change, you see, and it will not serve you if everyone you named as potential pallbearers or ministers have died when your time comes, or if they are physically incapable of the task.

What follows is a distillation of numerous professional pre-planning checklists and data sheets, along with some fiscal considerations. Take your time, make your phone calls and visits, and do as much as possible while in an up-beat frame of mind. If it starts dragging you down, leave it for a while or go on to another section—**don't let emotions overrule your practicality**.

Getting a mate's or relative's input can be valuable, but it's ***your*** decision that counts. It's ***your funeral***, right? The minor depression you may feel during the process will weigh lightly against the sense of accomplishment and peace of mind you'll feel having the arrangement decisions set down in writing.

First Step: Let Someone Know about This!

It will do you little good to plan if, when the time comes, no one knows where to find these plans! Let lots of people (especially your lawyer and next-of-kin) know where you keep these details, and keep them somewhere accessible, like in the family Bible or with other important papers.

THINK! If your plans are kept in a safe, who has access to it and the combination? If they are kept in a bank safety deposit box, at ***which bank*** and where are the keys? Also, what if death occurs Friday after banking hours? Will it be Monday (after all major decisions have been made) before anyone can get at these instructions?

You can make copies of the instructions and mail them to various relatives and friends, if you like, but some of this will be rather personal so you might want to limit access. However you decide to do it, make certain someone (preferably ***several*** people) knows where to find it. You can use this section, tear it from the book and have it enlarged at any copier shop (Kinko's) or leave it next to your cereal bowl if you wish, so long as those who will need the information know where to find it.

And that brings us to the first entries. Get a pencil and get busy, then send this first page to several friends and family members. You can (with our blessings) photocopy the planning section and update your forms when required. Just remember to destroy the out-dated copies.

In the Event of My Death

Name: ______________________________

Instructions for my Funeral and Disposition of my Remains are located:

____

____

____

To access, call: ____________(name) at (phone #)
(____)-_____-______

________________________ ________________________
[signature] [signature]

________________________ ________________________
[name, printed] [name, printed]

STEP TWO: DATA SHEET

Make as many copies as you like of the following form, to fill out as changes may occur later. This data sheet is a sort of life summary and a good place to list those things of which you are most proud. There is a discussion of it following the forms, but principally this form tells the reader who you are, what you've done, and what you would like done when the time comes.

Name: ______________________________________
(Current legal or married name)

Name: ______________________________________
(As I'd like it to appear in the Obituary)

Address: ___________________________________
____
____

Date of Birth: ____/____/____

Place of Birth: ______________________________

Previous Residence (s): ______________________
____
____

Military Service:
(Branch & Dates)

____
____
____
____

(Awards/Decorations)

____
____
____
____
____

Occupation: ______________________________
Company: ______________________________
How Long? __________
Education:
(Institution, Degree, Year)

____
____
____
____
____

Clubs/Fraternal Organizations:
(Include offices held, etc)

____
____
____
____

Social/Civic Organizations:

____
____
____

Hobbies/Interests:

____
____
____

Additional Information:

____
____
____

Marital Status & Spouse's Name: ____________________
(Include maiden name, if applicable)

Mother's Maiden Name: ____________________
Father's Name: ____________________

Siblings:

____
____
____
____

Children:

____
____
____
____
____
____
____

Grandchildren: (Use back of sheet if needed)

____
____
____
____
____
____
____
____
____
____

Number of Great Grandchildren: ______

On My Tombstone I Wish My Name to Read:

____

Color/Size/Style of Stone or Bronze Plaque:

____

Inscription to Read:

____

____

____

(Put these forms in a safe location)

That's the basic data sheet from which the obituary can be crafted, unless you'd like to tackle that yourself, which is not that difficult and the only way you'll know for sure what is said. Newspapers tend to keep a 'future file' of prewritten obituaries for celebrities and public figures, you can ask if they'd keep yours on file and update it periodically as needed.

I suggest you PRINT all information on this form clearly or type it. This is merely a skeleton; you can flesh-out the information as suits you using additional sheets just by writing SEE ATTACHED in the appropriate block. Your newspaper may have a standard form they use for obituaries and you can request a copy of this and fill it in as you see fit. Feel free to re-draft the data sheet in any manner you like, but make sure the cited information, as a minimum, is available.

Next, we'll get to Step 3, the gist of preplanning, the MEMORIAL PREFERENCES section, wherein you tell others what you have done and where you've done it. Make as many copies of these pages as you need, plus a few extras for later additions and updates. Bear in mind that each line completed on these forms represents considerable thought and research and will be one less decision that has to be made by survivors. They'll thank you for this.

MY MEMORIAL PREFERENCES

In preparation for the inevitable, I have reasoned and researched the possibilities and decided upon the following:

Cemetery Preference:

____

I (*HAVE/HAVE NOT*) purchased a plot/crypt space. If so, the paperwork is attached to this document or included with my personal papers that can be found here: ____

Disposition of my remains:
____Ground Burial
____Entombment (mausoleum)
____Cremation
____ Donation to Medical Science
In the case of cremation, I wish my ashes:
____ Retained in an urn.
____ Scattered (where?) ________________________
____ Scattered at-Sea.

Funeral Home Preference:

____

Pre-planning/pre-purchase documents are located:

____

I wish my memorial or funeral service to be:
____ Private (family only)____Public

If available, I would prefer my service be conducted by one of the following clergy in order of preference:

1.
2.

I would like my pallbearers selected from the following list (as their physical health and availability will allow):

____________________	____________________
____________________	____________________
____________________	____________________
____________________	____________________
____________________	____________________
____________________	____________________
____________________	____________________
____________________	____________________
____________________	____________________
____________________	____________________

My religious Denomination is: ____________________

My Church of preference is: ____________________

In lieu of Flowers, I would like acknowledgements made to:

____

____

____

I would prefer the following hymns &/or scriptures for my service:

____

____

____

____

I would like a eulogy delivered by:

____

Other Instructions Include:

____
____
____
____
____
____
____
____
____
____
____
____
____
____
____
____
____
____
____
____
____
____
____
____
____
____
____
____
____
____

FRIENDS & RELATIVES CONTACT LIST

(Make additional copies as needed)

Name: ______________________ Phones (home) ________
Address: ____________________ (work) ________
____________________ (cell) ________
Email: __________@______________
Relationship: ____________________________________

Name: ______________________ Phones (home) ________
Address: ____________________ (work) ________
____________________ (cell) ________
Email: __________@______________
Relationship: ____________________________________

Name: ______________________ Phones (home) ________
Address: ____________________ (work) ________
____________________ (cell) ________
Email: __________@______________
Relationship: ____________________________________

Name: ______________________ Phones (home) ________
Address: ____________________ (work) ________
____________________ (cell) ________
Email: __________@______________
Relationship: ____________________________________

Name: ______________________ Phones (home) ________
Address: ____________________ (work) ________
____________________ (cell) ________
Email: __________@______________
Relationship: ____________________________________

Name: ______________________ Phones (home) ________
Address: ____________________ (work) ________
____________________ (cell) ________
Email: __________@______________
Relationship: ____________________________________

Name: ______________________ Phones (home) ________
Address: ______________________ (work) ________
______________________ (cell) ________
Email: ___________@____________
Relationship: ______________________________

Name: ______________________ Phones (home) ________
Address: ______________________ (work) ________
______________________ (cell) ________
Email: ___________@____________
Relationship: ______________________________

Name: ______________________ Phones (home) ________
Address: ______________________ (work) ________
______________________ (cell) ________
Email: ___________@____________
Relationship: ______________________________

Name: ______________________ Phones (home) ________
Address: ______________________ (work) ________
______________________ (cell) ________
Email: ___________@____________
Relationship: ______________________________

Name: ______________________ Phones (home) ________
Address: ______________________ (work) ________
______________________ (cell) ________
Email: ___________@____________
Relationship: ______________________________

Name: ______________________ Phones (home) ________
Address: ______________________ (work) ________
______________________ (cell) ________
Email: ___________@____________
Relationship: ______________________________

Name: ______________________ Phones (home) ________
Address: ____________________ (work) ________
____________________ (cell) ________
Email: ____________@____________
Relationship: ________________________________

Name: ______________________ Phones (home) ________
Address: ____________________ (work) ________
____________________ (cell) ________
Email: ____________@____________
Relationship: ________________________________

Name: ______________________ Phones (home) ________
Address: ____________________ (work) ________
____________________ (cell) ________
Email: ____________@____________
Relationship: ________________________________

Name: ______________________ Phones (home) ________
Address: ____________________ (work) ________
____________________ (cell) ________
Email: ____________@____________
Relationship: ________________________________

Name: ______________________ Phones (home) ________
Address: ____________________ (work) ________
____________________ (cell) ________
Email: ____________@____________
Relationship: ________________________________

Documents:

Obviously, it would be wise for you to have a Last Will & Testament or something similar. Here would be the place to alert relatives of its existence, along with its location. (Yes, in addition to your basic info sheet) Additionally, there are other documents you may want to have accessible (i.e. your DD214, insurance policies, etc.) so feel free to duplicate this page and make their whereabouts known.

My attorney is: ______________________________
Phone: ___________________ Has copy of will? Y N
Address: ___________________________________

I Have BANK ACCOUNTS at the following institutions:

Bank: ____________________________________
Account Number: ___________________________

Bank: ____________________________________
Account Number: ___________________________

Bank: ____________________________________
Account Number: ___________________________

Bank: ____________________________________
Account Number: ___________________________

Bank: ____________________________________
Account Number: ___________________________

I have a SAFE DEPOSIT BOX at the following institution(s):

____

____

____

The keys are located:

____

IMPORTANT PAPERS ARE LOCATED:

Passports:

Last Will & Testament:

Birth Certificates:

Marriage License:

Military Discharge/DD214:

Deeds & Titles:

____

____

____

____

____

-

Mortgages & Notes:

____

____

____

____

____

Stocks & Bonds:

____
____
____
____
____

Income Tax Records_

____
____

Insurance Policies:

____
____

My Social Security Number: ____ - ___ - _____

MY Veterans Affairs Claim Number is: C-__________

Other:

____
____
____
____
____
____
____
____
____
____
____
____

PERSONAL BEQUESTS:

Even if you have a Last Will & Testament, chances are good there are some things that aren't specified. Perhaps they are keepsakes or maybe things you've acquired since your last up-date. Here's a chance to make your wishes known, though please understand this will not likely have the force of a Will. For legal advice contact your lawyer.

PERSONAL BEQUESTS

ARTICLE	BENEFICIARY

NOTE: PLEASE! Include preferred disposition of pets and houseplants. They have given you company and pleasure and deserve to be cared for after you're gone.

SCAMS

I don't care for the fact that there are vultures out there waiting to take advantage of a grieving family but feel it would do you, the reader, a great disservice not to address them. These ***Jackals***, as they are often called in crime-fighting arenas, have been around as long as there has been death in the civilized world.

They descend upon the survivors, either in person, by mail, or via telemarketing at a point when resistance is low and offer something personal for a price. They may even provide the item or service, but it is rarely what you expect and is often at an obscenely inflated price.

One of the oldest scams is the ***Gold-leaf Bible***. In the old days a traveling salesman would blow into town, check out the local obituaries to find a likely victim then show up on the front porch with a Bible bearing the deceased's name in gold print on its cover. ***"He wanted you to have this, I'm sure, to remember him always. He only owes X dollars on it and, if you can manage that balance, I'd love to present it to you right now."*** Millions of Bibles were sold this way.

Things have since gotten much more sophisticated. With today's computers and telemarketing schemes, literally billions of dollars can be bilked from the unwary in the days following a loss.

Consider this, the survivors will be receiving (and paying) bills for goods and services they don't encounter often. This includes bills related to both the funeral service and, likely as not, medical/hospital services preceding the death.

The thing that makes the survivors most vulnerable, of course, is the fact that they will likely be receiving insurance proceeds at about the same time, so an extra bill here or there won't hit as hard (or examined as closely) as it might be another time.

This plays on the old salesman's ploy that, once you get a customer (or pigeon) to signing things or saying ***Yes***, it is easier to slip one more thing in for approval. What if, while going through the pile of bills to be paid in the days and weeks following the loss of a family member, you stumble upon a bill for ***Hospital Chaplain Services .. $27.50*** or ***Gravesite Survey and Permit .. $47.10*** or ***Mid-State Medical Laboratory ..$37.45?***

Compared with other bills you are paying, these seem modest enough and, given the other unusual things you've encountered lately (Statements of Death AND Death Certificates) they sound legitimate. And yet, possibly none of them exist except in the demented minds of scam artists.

These bills will come from some entity with a likely-sounding name (***Hospital Chaplain's Corps, please make checks payable to H.C.C.,* or *M. Rumbold & Associates, Surveyors***) and include a pre-addressed envelope with a Post Office Box in a neighboring city. A rule of thumb: **if there's not a phone number included where you can verify charges, don't pay it!** You can also check with your funeral director and the hospital about any charges you are unsure of and, should you stumble upon a scam in progress, notify both the police and the post office.

I was taken for one of these following the death of my sons, albeit on a small scale. It was laminated copies of their obituary at, upon reflection, an outrageous price. Had I asked my funeral director, which I subsequently did, these were available through him at 1/10th the price. They arrived via the mail, along with a bill and a note that said, "***Someone who cares thought you might appreciate these. If not, please return them in the envelope provided.***" Per Federal law, I would have been within my rights to just keep the things without paying for them (since I had not requested them) but I appreciated the gesture and swallowed the bait.

A point to take home about these scams is that technology has obviated the need for the Big Con. We are so accessible, via direct mail, 'spam' email and phone lists, that even a small amount from each 'pigeon' multiplies quickly when spread among the 2,000,000+ families experiencing a loss each year. Watch your mail and monitor your phone ... they might be out to get you. If you have access to the Internet, you can check our Funeral Help website at ***www.funeral-help.com*** for more information on scams reported by consumers. If you encounter a novel scam, let us know and we'll help get the word out.

Be wary of anyone contacting you about an insurance policy the deceased allegedly has of which you have no knowledge. They might request a ***Processing Fee*** to forward the death benefits. **Legitimate insurance companies don't do this.** The same goes for companies that contact you, usually by phone, offering to streamline your Social Security or VA benefits or some other form of payment in return for a processing or release fee.

Oh, a final word on scams; an out-of-state monument company may contact you in the months following the loss of a loved one. Be aware that the mere shipment of granite runs about $19 per 100 pounds, so long distance sales are not generally profitable unless the prices are inflated or the quality low. You'll want to see and touch the stone you choose.

SUMMARY

The planning section of this book is perhaps the most important; put the information in one place so those left behind don't have to guess at what you wanted in the way of goods and services. If you do nothing else in the way of planning, please do your loved ones an immense favor and take the time to fill this out. The more specific you are, the less stress will be put on them when deciding what is to be done and who is to do it.

For those of you who are 'wired' into the Internet, please visit the **Funeral Help Program** at ***www.funeral-help.com*** or e-mail us at ***admin@funeral-help.com***. The site covers items on the funeral industry and arrangements, along with a range of other sources of useful information.

If you find this book omitted an area you feel needs addressing, or if you find some aspect was not covered as completely as you would like, please let me know. I hope to update this work periodically as conditions, laws, trends, and costs dictate, and reissue it as a new edition to better serve those who need it. Also, if you find a particular section beneficial I'd appreciate hearing about this, too. I can be reached at:

Dr. R. E. Markin
The Funeral Help Program (FHP)
1236 Ginger Crescent
Virginia Beach, VA 23453
Toll free: 877-427-0220

Good luck.

APPENDIX A

SOURCES, CONTACTS & ORGANIZATIONS

VETERANS SOURCES:

BURIAL AT-SEA

Retired Activities Section (Pers-62)
Bureau of Naval Personnel
Washington, D.C., 20370-6620
Phone: 1-703-614-3197

(For Retirees)
Officer in Charge
Attn: Mortuary Affairs Section
Military Medical Support Office
PO Box 886999
Great Lakes, IL 60088-6999
Phone: 1-888-647-6676, select option 4

Commandant (G-PMP-2)
Coast Guard Group Miami
100 MacArthur Causeway
Miami Beach, FL 33139
(305) 535-4111

U.S Coast Guard
2100 Second St., S.W.
Washington, D.C. 20593-0001
Phone: 1-800-772-8724 or 1-202-267-2257

BURIAL IN NATIONAL CEMETERIES

Superintendent,
Arlington National Cemetery
Arlington, VA 22211-5003
Phone: 1-703-607-8585

INFORMATION REQUIRED FOR BURIAL IN NATIONAL CEMETERY

* Full name and military grade
* Uniformed Service (Branch)
* Social Security Number
* Service number (if applicable and known)
* VA claim number (if assigned and known)
* Date and place of birth
* Date of retirement or honorable separation from active duty
* Date and place of death
* Copy of separation papers, such as DD Form 214

VA FLAG (for veteran's casket, presentation to family)

Available from VA with completed VA FORM 2008
Also available from many post offices
Phone: 1-800-827-1000

PRESIDENTIAL MEMORIAL CERTIFICATES (PMC) PROGRAM
Apply at nearest VA Regional Office

VA TRANSPORTATION AND BURIAL ALLOWANCE

Contact nearest VA Regional Office to inquire as to eligibility. Many new constraints have been placed upon these allowances in recent years, but anyone receiving (or qualified to receive) disability should investigate. Allowances run $150, $300, or $1500.00.

VA HEADSTONES & MARKERS

Office of Memorial Programs (403)
Department of Veteran Affairs
810 Vermont Avenue NW
Washington, D.C. 20420
Phone: 1-800-697-6947
Ask for Form 40-1330 [some funeral directors can provide this form]

ANATOMICAL GIFTS (Donating one's body to science)

Uniformed Services University of Health Sciences
4301 Jones Bridge Road
Bethesda, MD 20814-4799
Phone: (301) 295-3333
Also, virtually any medical school and/or teaching hospital.

MILITARY HONORS

Virtually anyone who served on active duty in the military can receive graveside honors including a rifle salute, the playing of *Taps* by a bugler, and the flag ceremony. Phone the nearest military base (including ROTC and Recruiting Stations) or veterans organization. The American Legion, Veterans of Foreign Wars (VFW), and American Veterans (AMVETS) can either provide or direct you to these services.

CONSUMER SOURCES OF INFORMATION

"Product Report: *Prepaying Your Funeral*?" (D13188)
AARP Fulfillment (EE0139)
601 E Street NW
Washington, D.C. 20049
(Send a postcard and allow six weeks for delivery of this very detailed and informative report)

Federal Trade Commission, Funeral Rule
Attention: Public Reference Branch
Room 130
6th Street and Pennsylvania Avenue, N.W.
Washington, D.C. 20580
(Get the inside skinny on exactly what the funeral industry is *supposed* to be telling you by requesting these Funeral Rule Requirements)

Cremation Association of North America
401 N. Michigan Avenue
Chicago, IL 60611
Phone: (312) 245-1077
(Send a self-addressed envelope with 75-cents postage to receive six informative pamphlets on cremation as an alternative to burial)

International Order of the Golden Rule
P.O. Box 28689
St. Louis, MO 63146-1189
Phone: 1-800-637-8030
[An association of about 1500 independent funeral homes. The emphasis is on 'independent' and membership is by invitation-only. Good source of information on the family-owned segment of industry without the corporate 'spin' you'll get from SCI]

'It's Your Choice'
AARP Books
Scott Foresman & Company
1865 Miner Street
Des Plaines, IL 60016
(This is a good book to assist in preplanning. The cost is $4.95 ($3.00 if you are a member of AARP) plus $1.75 postage and handling)

Jewish Funeral Directors of America, Inc.
Seaport Landing, 150 Lynnway Suite 506
Lynn, MA 01902
Phone: (781) 477-9300 (closed on Passover)
[JFDA is the national trade association of the Jewish funeral director community. Approximately 200 members. Since the traditional Jewish burial is extremely practical and cost-effective, this could be an excellent source of information on reasonable caskets, etc]

National Funeral Directors and Morticians Association
3951 Snapfinger Parkway, Suite 570
Omega World Center
Decatur, GA 30035
Phone: (800) 434-0958
[NFDMA is the national association of Black funeral directors and has some 2000 members.]

SOCIAL SECURITY BENEFITS

There is a standard $255.00 burial benefit, in addition to a range of benefits for survivors. Contact your local Social Security Office for the proper forms and requirements. You will need a copy of the Statement of Death By Funeral Director (sometimes called a Death Report) and the funeral director in many cases will file this for you.

DONATING ORGANS

The Living Bank
P.O. Box 6725
Houston, TX 77265
Phone: (713) 528-2971
OR
YOUR LOCAL HOSPITAL
[Virtually any hospital can either service this request and supply the required forms, or refer you to an organ bank that can]
OR
YOUR NEAREST HOSPICE
[Hospices are becoming more sophisticated all the time and *can be* a valuable source for information on both organ/tissue donation and anything related to death and dying. BEWARE! *I encountered numerous hospices which have **funeral directors** as members of their Boards of Directors, so you might take anything from a hospice with a grain of salt or a little research.*]

CONSUMER SOURCES FOR DISCOUNT INFORMATION & PRICES

F.H.P. (Funeral Help Program)
1236 Ginger Crescent
Virginia Beach, VA 23453
Phone 1-877-427-0220
Email: admin@funeral-help.com
For copies of this book/program, call 1-757-427-0220 8 am-10 pm EST
[Free screening of potential savings areas, as well as casket/vault/urn national cost comparison and referral to someone who can provide same unit at significant savings.]
Also available by Internet at www.funeral-help.com

Donations in Lieu of Flowers

The ***Funeral Help Program*** grew out of a grant from the Alzheimer's Research Foundation. We think it only fitting to mention their motto, as depicted on their acknowledgement cards; "***the gift of hope outlasts any flower***." Flowers do fade quickly, cost a small fortune, and cannot be appreciated by the 'guest of honor'. If you wish to have friends and family make donations to their favorite cause in lieu of flowers, be sure and mention this in the death notice or obituary and brief the funeral director so he'll know when friends call.

APPENDIX B
CHECKLISTS

Funeral Arrangements, General

- Friend (contact and get by your side)
- Notifying Friends and Family (initiate call tree)
- Choosing a Service (memorial or funeral? Graveside, church, or funeral home chapel?)
- The 'End Site' (Ground burial, mausoleum, cremation? Does deceased have a site? Check newspapers/ad papers, call around. Are vaults required? Price? Restrictions on monuments? Visitation?) Compare grave cost with mausoleum.
- Selecting A Funeral Home: (Call, request price sheets. Visit, view caskets, get quotes on models, colors and interiors, call FHP for free price comparison*.)

NOTE: You can probably buy casket, urn, and vaults at a savings of 30% to 60% (average) by calling 1-877-427-0220, give the model number over phone, and get cost comparison from a nationwide bank of providers who can provide any model delivered within hours.

Review Funeral Home Information, make choice of services.
Select Casket, order
Paperwork requirements (copies of Death Cert., etc...)

NOTE: You will need a certified copy of the *Death Certificate* (vs. the Statement of Death by Funeral Director) for EACH insurance policy as well as for your own records. Social Security, IRS, etc ... will accept the Statement of Death)

The obituary (see pre-planning section covering personal information)
Acknowledgments (floral, other, instructions)
Transfer of Remains

(If out of state, request NMS handle transfer through selected funeral home which will be receiving the remains)

Check on deceased's pets and houseplants!
Choose a Vault (Call for cost comparison)
The PRELUDE:

Viewing periods (how many, when? Cost?)
Common Areas (Kitchen, lounge)
Food & Coffee (Disposable cups, plates, etc)

Planning the service: How long will it be? Format? Contact minister
Which hymns? Who will ride with whom? Who will need assistance?

Opening and Closing the Grave (Get prices per day/time)
Military Service (See Veterans Section in Appendix A)
How to Pay (Was there a prepaid plan? Insurance? Does Credit Plan allow carry-over until life insurance benefits arrive? Accept Credit Cards?)

Getting Benefits (VA & Social Security, filing for insurance claims, get copies of Statement of Death, Death Certificate, DD214, etc... *Quite often the funeral director will file these forms for you.*)

ONCE IT'S OVER: TAKE SOME TIME OUT FOR YOURSELF!

Once the funeral is over, go somewhere or do something to distance yourself from your grief and the stress of the past few days. Visit an old friend, take a short tour, or just book yourself into a nice Bed & Breakfast in the country, but do get away for a few days. You'll be glad you did.

The Week After:

- Decide what to do with pets, houseplants
- Contact lawyer, check for 'loose ends'
- Thank You cards and phone acknowledgments
- Optional Gratitude Announcement in newspaper
- Watch mail for scams/opportunists

Months Later: Choosing a monument:

- Visit Cemeteries, look for tags on monuments.
- Visit monument yards (Price stones, ask about grade of granite used)
- Get print-outs with information on 'stone' to balance information.
- Apply for VA monument. (makes a nice 'footstone', even if you buy another headstone . . . and it's *free!)*

NOTES